W9-AAT-908

The Waverly Gallery

By the same author

This Is Our Youth

KENNETH LONERGAN

The Waverly Gallery

Grove Press
New York

Copyright © 2000 by Kenneth Lonergan

All rights reserved. No part of this book may be reproduced in any form or by any electronic or mechanical means, including information storage and retrieval systems, without permission in writing from the publisher, except by a reviewer, who may quote brief passages in a review. Any members of educational institutions wishing to photocopy part or all of the work for classroom use, or publishers who would like to obtain permission to include the work in an anthology, should send their inquiries to Grove/Atlantic, Inc., 841 Broadway, New York, NY 10003.

CAUTION: Professionals and amateurs are hereby warned that *The Waverly Gallery* is subject to a royalty. It is fully protected under the copyright laws of the United States, Canada, United Kingdom, and all British Commonwealth countries, all countries covered by the International Copyright Union, the Pan-American Copyright Convention, the Universal Copyright Convention, or the Berne Convention, and all countries with which the United States has reciprocal copyright relations. All rights, including professional, amateur, motion picture, recitation, public reading, radio broadcasting, television, and video or sound taping, all other forms of mechanical or electronic reproduction, such as information storage and retrieval systems and photocopying, and rights of translation into foreign languages are strictly reserved. In its present form the play is dedicated to the reading public only.

All inquiries concerning English language stock and amateur applications for permission to perform the play must be made in advance to Samuel French, Inc., 45 West 25th Street, New York, NY 10010. No professional or nonprofessional performance of the play may be given without obtaining in advance the written permission of Dramatists Play Service and paying the requisite fee, whether the play is presented for charity or gain and whether or not admission is charged. First-class professional applications for permission to perform the play, and for those other rights stated above, must be made in advance to William Morris Agency, Inc., 1325 Avenue of the Americas, New York, NY 10019, ATTN. George Lane.

Printed in the United States of America

ISBN 0-7394-1318-X

This play is dedicated to my grandmother and my mother.

FOREWORD

SMALL THEATERS, BIG PLAYS

In order to talk about a playwright whose work I find exquis-
itely sensitive and nuanced, I would like to take a moment for
nostalgia for What Was. (You cannot talk about the theater
in the year 2000, I find, without being at least a little nostal-
gic.) In the late 1980s, there occurred in the New York
theater a little growth spurt, a mushrooming of small companies: I am referring in particular to The Atlantic Theatre
Company, Malaparte, and Naked Angels, all of them being
three notable venues for writing or acting on any given fall or
winter night. Naked Angels (where for a minute and a half I
was hapless coartistic director) occupied a former picture-
framing factory on West Seventeenth Street. It was ruled by
the actors (the high school equivalent of the jocks). There
was a little cabal of writers (the nerds) including Kenny
Lonergan, Frank Pugliesse, and myself (seldom in agreement),
plotting in corners to put on shows and take control of the
place—frankly an impossible task, as Naked Angels was as
much a roving gang of anarchistic factions as it was a theater
company. It was an exciting and volatile place, one part
Steppenwolf, one part Circle Rep, three parts Tower of Babel.

What was especially exciting for me was to watch one's peers make useful discoveries and to grow as artists, in an environment that generally excluded critics and reviewers. There were openhearted young audiences, who seemed vivid and happy to be there (unlike the subscribers at some of the more established local institutions, where it often seemed that the jaded and the tired went for a night out between dinner and the eleven o'clock news).

I mention the above because I think of all the playwrights to come out of that time and place, there is no one who took better advantage of the resources of a small company than Kenny Lonergan. He is an argument for the importance of small theater companies to the health of the American theater. It was at Naked Angels that he developed his voice as an artist. Week after week, at our Works in Progress series, Kenny would try out scraps and scenes and pages and bits. He would write for actors, and for the ears of other writers. I think there are some playwrights who come into the world fully formed and ready to spill out their work. Kenny is not one of them. He is like most of the rest of us: in fits and starts, his voice got louder and clearer and more refined. The outline that developed was strong and idiomatic. The characters he wrote were all parts of the Kenny Lonergan of the time: the recessive, the under-achiever, the bright but inarticulate, the mismatched baleful lover, the melancholic champion of the underdog—these were the most overtly visible traits (and I mean this only as a compliment, I assure you). The first time I saw all of those qualities unified in his work was in the early Naked Angels version of *This Is Our Youth*. I'll never forget it. It was as though all those scraps and monologues and sketches and scenes of Kenny's from *Angels in Progress* or our *Issues Projects* had come together in one play. I realized then that beyond just writing from an easy affection for his characters, Kenny writes from a deep and troubled and true love for them.

Which brings me with profound pleasure and even awe to *The Waverly Gallery*. It is in this play that we see what happens after youth passes into maturity; the result is a vividly compassionate family play written with incomparable veracity and built on a delicate armature of memory and regret. It is a play about the slow-motion moment in a family when that which has been merely gnawing and difficult becomes tragic. It is also (as in life, and all of Kenny's work) filled with a wry and hilarious comedy. Kenny understands something Chekhov and Lanford Wilson know: that mere human yearning to live a little longer (and perhaps a little better) can be a more powerful passion than lust or even vengeance. It has staying power, and it's instantly recognizable. He is a humanist. He has no ideology or agenda. The narrative of life as your parents and loved ones reach the end is tragic and it happens to all of us. But it breaks your heart when rendered as honestly as it is in this play. In *The Waverly Gallery*, life is slipping away. Meet Gladys Green, once a firebrand Greenwich Village Bohemian of the kind that is now virtually extinct, now growing deaf and—more alarming—terrifyingly forgetful. There is a growing blankness and fretfulness in the ever-widening chasms between her good cheer and resilience. There is an increasing panic as Gladys's family struggles for continuity and grace—and a solution (impossible), to the sad reality of watching someone you love disappear before your eyes. As I watched the play knowing it was an intensely autobiographical piece, it occurred to me that all those years ago at Naked Angels, Kenny Lonergan was busy living the drama he was preparing to write as grown-up artist. I am proud we shared and continue to share the same boards.

Jon Robin Baitz
New York City
September 2000

The world premiere of *The Waverly Gallery* was originally produced by the Williamstown Theatre Festival; Michael Ritchie, Producer. It was presented on August 11, 1999 with the following cast:

Gladys Green	Eileen Heckart
Ellen Fine	Maureen Anderman
Daniel Reed	Josh Hamilton
Howard Fine	Mark Blum
Don Bowman	Anthony Arkin
Alan George	Stephen Mendillo

Directed by Scott Ellis

The Waverly Gallery was produced on the New York stage by Anita Waxman, Elizabeth Williams, Randall L. Wreghitt, Peggy Lieber, and Eric Lieber, in association with Second Stage Theatre. *The Waverly Gallery* was presented in New York, New York on March 27, 2000, at the Promenade Theatre with the following cast:

Gladys Green	Eileen Heckart
Ellen Fine	Maureen Anderman
Daniel Reed	Josh Hamilton
Howard Fine	Mark Blum
Don Bowman	Anthony Arkin
Gladys Green (matinee performances)	Scotty Bloch

Directed by Scott Ellis

Scenery design by Derek McLane, costumes by Michael Krass, lighting by Kenneth Posner, sound by Bruce Ellman, original music by Jason Robert Brown, and casting by Amy Chistopher. The production stage manager was Lloyd Davis, Jr.

CHARACTERS

Gladys Green   A former lawyer and Greenwich Village activist, runs a small art gallery, eighties

Ellen Fine   Her daughter, a psychiatrist, fifties

Daniel Reed   Ellen's son, a speechwriter, twenties

Howard Fine   Ellen's husband, Daniel's stepfather, a psychiatrist, fifties

Don Bowman   A painter and waiter from Lynn, Massachusetts, thirties

The Play takes place in New York City, in Greenwich Village and on the Upper West Side of Manhattan, between 1989 and 1991.

Simultaneous Dialogue

For characters speaking to each other, double dialogue laid out in side-by-side columns is meant to be spoken *simultaneously*. I.e., the actor saying the dialogue in the right-hand column is *not* to wait for the actor saying the dialogue in the left-hand column to finish, but to speak at the exact same time, taking his cue from the *vertical* placement of the text.

For example:

CHARACTER A	
What do you mean, speak at the same time? Didn't we—	
I *am* speaking at the same	CHARACTER B
time—	They mean speak *simulta-*
Well *you* didn't do it.	*neously.*
	Don't wait for—That's not the point.

In the above, Character B says the word "They" at the same time that Character A says the word "I" and the word "Don't" at the same time Character A says the word "Well."

HOWEVER, for double columns in which *two sets* of characters are having separate but simultaneous conversations, the speakers *start* at the same time, but continue along only in reference to their own column.

For example:

CHARACTER A	CHARACTER C
I saw that movie yesterday.	What time does the bus get in?

CHARACTER B	CHARACTER D
Oh yeah? Was it good?	Five o'clock.
CHARACTER A	CHARACTER C
No, not especially.	The bus gets in at five o'clock?

In the above, Characters A and C start speaking at the same time, but then each column proceeds at its own pace, without reference to the other column.

While in some cases absolute precision is neither possible nor necessary, in general, the more precisely the actors try to stick to these rules, the better the double dialogue will work.

ACT ONE, SCENE ONE

A tiny gallery in Greenwich Village in the fall of 1989. GLADYS GREEN and her grandson DANIEL REED sit on either side of Gladys' desk, eating sandwiches. Gladys is 85, extremely energetic and very hard of hearing. She wears a hearing aid that doesn't do her much good. She is an extraordinarily garrulous, immensely charming and absolutely relentless talker who covers her deep and secret embarrassment at her deafness with even more talking. She lives for company and conversation and perhaps because of her advancing years demands the full attention of her interlocutors with a cheerful and unremitting zeal that can be very wearing after a few minutes. Daniel is a very bright, occasionally shy, occasionally sarcastic young man with a sense of humor sometimes described as dry. He is at present giving Gladys his more or less friendly attention.

GLADYS   I never knew anything was the matter. Your mother never told me anything. And then one day your father calls me on the phone and says he's coming by to say good-bye and that he's moving out. And I said, "I don't understand! What happened?" But he wouldn't tell me, and neither would your mother. I called her and I said, "What is the matter?" But she just said that your father had left her and that's all I ever knew about it. We always liked Mark, everybody did, but we felt so bad for him, you know . . . His mother was a little kooky, you know? She was charming as hell, but she never knew what to do with him. I *liked* her, but she was a nut, she was meshugge. Do you know what that word means?

DANIEL   Yes, I know what it means.

GLADYS   What?

DANIEL   I SAID I KNOW WHAT IT MEANS.

GLADYS   It means kooky, you know: a little nutty—And you know your father never had a real father of his own. But your father and your grandfather, Herb—my husband— were very close. He put your father through medical school, you know—

DANIEL   Yes, I know . . .

GLADYS   And he said to your father that he would pay for his medical school whether he married Ellen or not. And he also paid for Mark to be in treatment, you know, with a psychiatrist—

DANIEL   Yeah, I know.

GLADYS   And Mark loved that doctor, but he died too. And your poor father just stood there by the window, crying. I never saw anything like it. He was absolutely heartbroken. Because you know he never had a father of his own, not really. But we always liked Mark. He's a hell of a nice guy, he really is. His mother was witty as hell, but she was a kook, a nut, she was nutty. She had a little magazine, I think, that she used to publish. She was a rather good artist too, and she had a play on Broadway, and she had a very good sense of humor. Oh, she was very charming. But she just didn't know what to do with him. And your mother and father, you know, they were married in that same apartment, in the one, you know, the one in the back, the one you live in. They were married there, did you know that?

DANIEL   Yeah, I did.

GLADYS   What, honey?

DANIEL   YES, I KNEW THAT. I KNEW THAT.

GLADYS   We were very happy in that apartment. You know I built that apartment, when Herb and I—that's Herb, your grandfather, my husband—when we bought the building after we came back from Germany. You know we lived in Germany for two years, before the War, because Herb was studying in a laboratory there—

DANIEL   I know!

GLADYS   Well it's a beautiful apartment. Are you happy there, sweet?

DANIEL   Yes, very happy. I love it.

GLADYS   You love it. Well, that's wonderful. And have you got it all . . . fixed up the way you like it, honey?

DANIEL   Yes, I just got it painted!

GLADYS   Oh, I haven't seen what you did with it.

DANIEL   Yes you have. You've seen it since then.

GLADYS   What?

DANIEL   YOU'VE SEEN IT.

GLADYS   No, I don't think so.

DANIEL   You've seen it a few times. You don't remember.

GLADYS   Well, maybe I don't remember. But we were very happy there. Do you have a lot of parties?

DANIEL   Once in a while.

GLADYS   You do. Well that's wonderful.

DANIEL   No, once in a while! Not very often!

GLADYS   Well why not? You should have parties, we had parties all the time. We had a New Year's Eve party every year—

DANIEL   Well I'm not as much of a social b—

GLADYS   What?

DANIEL   I'm not as much of a social butterfly as you are!

She laughs and gives him a friendly slap on the wrist.

GLADYS   Well why not? Are you shy?

DANIEL   Yeah, I'm a little shy!

GLADYS   You're not shy, are you? Ellen is shy. Your mother is very shy—

DANIEL   Well, she gets it from you!

GLADYS (*Laughs again*)   From *me*? I was never shy, I love to talk to people! I was never shy! I never understood how your mother can be so shy. She's so beautiful, and she's such a good mother, and she's a damn good doctor. Do you know that, honey?

DANIEL   Yes, I know.

GLADYS   Well your grandfather—that's Herb, your grandfather, my husband—was a doctor too, you know. And he and I were very active in politics at that time. I was with the American Labor Party—Do you know what that is, honey?

DANIEL   Yeah, basically.

GLADYS   And Emily Bradshaw said that I should run on the ticket for City Council. Did you know that, honey?

DANIEL   Yes!

GLADYS   What?

DANIEL   I said I knew that! Hold on—(*He leans in to adjust her hearing aid.*)

GLADYS
No! Don't fiddle with it!
You're gonna break it!
What? This damn thing is
such a nuisance—What?

DANIEL
Just wait a minute . . .
Hold on. Stop talking
—Stop talking for
a second! (*He adjusts the
hearing aid.*)

DANIEL (*In a normal voice*)   Can you hear me?

She doesn't hear. He adjusts the hearing aid again.

DANIEL (*Softly*)   Can you hear me?

GLADYS   I can hear you, yes.

He sits back down. She starts to touch the hearing aid.

DANIEL   No, don't touch it! If you can hear me, leave it
alone.

She obediently puts her hands on the table.

GLADYS   I won't touch it.

DANIEL   OK.

She laughs and touches his cheek.

GLADYS   So are you working hard, honey? Are you working
too hard?

DANIEL   Not really.

GLADYS   Are you still . . . writing for the newspaper?

DANIEL   No, I don't write for a newspaper.

GLADYS   What?

DANIEL   I don't write for the newspaper.

GLADYS You don't. What do you do?

DANIEL I write speeches for the Environmental Protection Agency.

GLADYS Who reads them?

DANIEL No—I write for a politician, for the local head of the Environmental Protection Agency. It's a government agency—

GLADYS And do they get—do you get criticisms, critiques of them, do people see them? Who publishes them?

DANIEL No, they don't get published, somebody *gives* them . . . Somebody—

GLADYS Do you enjoy your work?

DANIEL Yes, I do.

GLADYS Well that's wonderful. That's absolutely marvelous. But if you ever need any money, you know you can always ask me, and you don't have to pay it back, in case you ever need some spare cash, and we don't have to say anything to your mother.

DANIEL No, that's all right. Thank you, but I'm all right.

GLADYS Well I'd *enjoy* giving it to you! Everybody needs money.

DANIEL That's true.

GLADYS What?

DANIEL I SAID THAT'S TRUE.

GLADYS Well sure it's true. We always had plenty of money, my father always had plenty of money, and then my brother Harold. But he was a real bastard, you know? Nobody ever

6

liked him. He just didn't know how to get along with people. But if you were ever in trouble, ever in real trouble, he would always lend you money. That's important . . .

DANIEL Sure . . . !

GLADYS Sure. Some people just—they don't know how to get along with people. They just don't know how. They're very troubled. Your father was so charming and so bright— you know he's very smart—but he was very troubled at that time. He couldn't help it. And Ellen was just crazy about him. But she never told me anything. I never knew anything.

DANIEL I know.

Daniel gets up abruptly and comes downstage, addressing the audience directly. Behind him Gladys slowly cleans up the sandwiches.

DANIEL (*To the audience*) I want to tell you what happened to my grandmother, Gladys Green, near the end of her life. I lived in her building—where I still live—in Greenwich Village, during the last couple of years when she was there. I live in the back apartment. She was in the front, just down the hall. My grandfather—Herb, her husband—died before I was born, and after that she lived with a man named Ronald, but then he died too, and after that she was by herself. For twenty-eight years she ran a tiny gallery on Waverly Place, around the corner from where we lived. And without being too depressing about it, she didn't always have the best stuff in there. But some of it was pretty good. Most days you could see her in there, watching television or looking out the window. I used to drop by once in a while, but usually if I was walking past the gallery, I'd just duck down behind the cars across the street so she wouldn't see me go by. Until her eyesight got really bad.

7

Then you could just walk right past the window. It's not that I didn't like her. I did. It's just that once you went in there, it was kind of tough getting out again. So I was pretty stingy with the visits.

The last person to have a show there was named Don Bowman, from Massachusetts. He came to the city with an expensive car and no money. He took his pictures into every gallery he could find, until he found my grandmother in the Waverly Gallery off Washington Square. (*Daniel exits.*)

ACT ONE, SCENE TWO

*In the little gallery, GLADYS is looking at Don Bowman's portfolio.
DON is in his mid-thirties, and speaks with a working-class Boston-
area accent. He is a little peculiar—and always slightly out of step
with those around him, a careful, hardworking and detail-fixated
person who devotes a lot of his mental energy to very slowly and
carefully arriving at the wrong conclusion.*

GLADYS You know, these are very good. You're a very good
   artist.

DON Yeah, that's my sister. That's her actual wheelchair . . .
   and that's her in her bedroom. You can't see it, but—

GLADYS These are absolutely marvelous.

DON —behind the bureau there's a ramp for her wheelchair,
   but the bureau interferes with the angle. That's her cat.

GLADYS And are you—you know, are you showing them
   around in the art galleries?

DON That's my mother . . .

GLADYS Another gallery?

DON (*Not loud enough*) No, that's my *mother.*

Gladys doesn't hear him.

GLADYS Uh-huh. Well, this show here has been up for a
   long time—the paintings are by a very talented artist whom
   I have known for many years. He lives in Europe now with
   a man—with his partner. And I told him when he left that I
   can't keep the pictures up for more than a few weeks, and
   he said, "That's OK, keep 'em up as long as you want!"
   (*She laughs*) But I'm in a jam! Because I don't know what to

do with them. I need someone to take them down. I can't do it myself.

DON Well—

GLADYS Are you over at—over at the school?

DON (*Laughs*) No, no, I'm not at—

GLADYS Well what's the matter? Don't you think it's a good school?

DON No, I—

GLADYS Are you a New Yorker?

DON No, I'm from New England.

GLADYS From New England, well it's very pretty up there. My daughter went to medical school in Boston. She lives up by the park—

DON Yeah, I'm from just outside of Boston. My mother still lives there. I don't really know anybody in New York. My sister lives in New Jersey—

GLADYS And my grandson is a—he's—you know, he writes—articles—for the newspaper. You should show him some of your pictures, maybe he'll—you know, maybe he'll write 'em up for you.

DON What paper does he write for?

She doesn't hear.

DON What paper does he write for?

She doesn't hear.

DON Does he—

GLADYS   Would you like to put some of your—your pictures up in here? We can put up a few and see what happens.

DON   Oh—Yes . . . ! Of course! That would be wonderful.

GLADYS   It's not a big place, but it's cute. You know? A lot of students come in here. They look around, and we talk, and a lot of them want to show me their work. There are a lot of good artists around, but they don't have anyone to help them. It's not a fancy place, but it's all right.

DON   No, I really like it. It has a lot of character.

GLADYS   I used to have a lot of shows in here, but I have a bad—foot, and I can't walk so well, so I don't come in as much as I used to. I've been on this corner for quite a few years now. I live right around the corner, and my grandson has the apartment in the back. I live in the front.

DON   Uh-huh . . .

GLADYS   I just walk over from my apartment, and I bring a little—sandwich. I have a little—television, that I like to watch sometimes. Something's wrong with it so I don't watch it anymore. But I come in and I read the paper, and I always keep that door locked, because you never know who the hell is going to come in these days. This whole neighborhood is changing. This one's sellin' drugs, and that one's tryin' to—get your money—and that one's boppin' people on the head. They have all kinds of signals, they have red hats and blue hats, and you can't tell one from the other, and there are a lot of people now from *South Korea*. They're very well dressed, they've got a lot of money, but that government they have doesn't let them—They don't want to live *there*. They want to come *here*. And the man who runs the hotel likes to have the gallery in the building because people stop by and look in. But he's redoing the whole place—

DON   Yeah, I saw the hotel was under construc—

GLADYS   Now if you want to put two or three pictures up, you'll have to hang them yourself—

DON   That's no problem—

GLADYS   And if you sell anything, the gallery takes fifty percent of the—of the sale. That's half and half. Now, I don't know what kind of prices you want to charge—

DON   All right. Now if I could—

GLADYS   What?

DON   (*Louder*)   I was just wondering if I could store the rest of the stuff somewhere around here—

GLADYS   Well sure, you can keep them in the back—

DON   —because I been drivin' back and forth to New Jersey and I don't like to have the pictures rattlin' around in the car every day. I work as a waiter up in Lynn, in Massachusetts, and my plan was to come down here and stay with my sister, but she's in a wheelchair, and her house is pretty small, and I didn't realize it's almost a two-hour drive each way, so—

GLADYS   Don't you have an apartment?

DON   No, I—

GLADYS   Well you can't sleep on the street!

DON   Well, last night I was too tired to drive all the way back, so I did actually sleep in the car, but—

GLADYS   In the car!

DON   Well the front seat reclines all the way back, so it wasn't really too bad—

GLADYS   Well I'll tell you what. You can buy yourself a little . . . cot. And I have a room in the back here, where I keep the pictures. Why don't you get yourself a little—you know, a little fold-out cot, and you can stay in the back there until you get yourself settled in. I only use the place in the day—I live right around the corner—Here, would you like to see it?

DON   Well . . . um . . .

GLADYS   I don't know if you'll be very comfortable—but it's better than sleeping on the street! Somebody's liable to come along and bop you on the head! This whole neighborhood is changing. There's always some racket outside. They're always setting things off or blowing somethin' up . . . This used to be a beautiful neighborhood. Now you don't know which one is on drugs and which one is *crazy* . . .

Don follows her as she makes her slow way toward the back.

DON   Well—if I could really—I mean, if you don't mind, that would be incredibly convenient—

GLADYS   Well why should I mind? I like helping young people. All they want is a little chance. But they don't have anyone to help them.

DON   I mean, eventually it would be great to have a whole show here . . .

Gladys stops walking so she can talk some more.

GLADYS   I don't come in very often. I never ran this place to make money. I'm a lawyer for many years, but I don't practice anymore. It just gives me something to do, you know? And I enjoy it. I really do. I've had some rather good artists in here . . . But if you want, we can take down all these pictures, because the artist is in—in Europe. I'm very angry at him because he left for Europe and he left me all these pictures! I don't know what to do with them. You have to change the show after a while because people walk by and they want to see something new. Do you have enough pictures to put up in here?

DON   Oh I've got more pictures than you want . . .

She doesn't hear. Pause.

DON   I say, I've probably got more pictures than you want.

GLADYS   Well why shouldn't I want them? I think they show a lot of talent. You're a very talented artist.

DON   Thank you. . . !

ACT ONE, SCENE THREE

Daniel enters as the lights cross-fade from the gallery to Ellen and Howard's kitchen across the stage. As Don exits the gallery, ELLEN and HOWARD FINE enter and sit at the kitchen table. Ellen is an Upper West Side psychiatrist and mother, shy with strangers, devoted to her family, but easily frazzled—especially by her mother, and particularly when she is frightened. Howard is a genial, loving, generous man, also a psychiatrist, who prides himself on being straightforward and practical—occasionally to the point of insensitivity.

(NOTE: *When the family speaks to Gladys they must always speak very loudly and clearly to be heard—but not too loud or her hearing aid whistles. Unless you are right next to her, she cannot really hear a normal tone of voice, even when the hearing aid is functioning properly.*)

GLADYS   Hello, honey. (*She grabs Daniel's face and kisses it.*) How are you, honey? All right?

DANIEL   Yes, I'm fine thanks.

GLADYS   What?

DANIEL   I said I'm fine!

GLADYS   Good. I'm glad.

DANIEL   Why don't you come in and have some dinner!

GLADYS   What?

DANIEL   I said come eat dinner!

Daniel and Gladys cross toward Ellen and Howard, who are at the table, mid-meal.

GLADYS   All right, honey, what are we having?

DANIEL   I'm not sure. I think we're having meat loaf!

GLADYS   We're not having chicken, are we?

DANIEL   No—we're having meat loaf.

GLADYS   I've had chicken three times already this week.

DANIEL (*Louder*)   We're not having chicken! We're having MEAT LOAF. MEAT LOAF.

GLADYS (*Still not hearing*)   Well, that's all right. Your mother is a wonderful cook.

Daniel sits Gladys at one end of the table, then sits between her and Ellen. Howard is at the other end.

GLADYS   That whole neighborhood is changing. (*To Daniel*) Honey? Do you think the Village has changed much in the last five years?

DANIEL   Yes! It's been changing for a lot longer than that!

GLADYS   The whole place is changing. And there are a lot of people now from South Korea.

ELLEN   What is this South *Korea* thing?

GLADYS They're everywhere you look! They're very well dressed, and they have a lot of money. They come in the gallery all the time. The whole neighborhood is changing.	**DANIEL** I guess a lot of the NYU students are Asian, but I don't really know . . .

DANIEL   Sure!

GLADYS   That bank around the corner used to be a very friendly bank. I knew the manager for many years, and it was always a very friendly place. Now, the whole place is black. The whole bank. It's all—*black*. And we *wanted* that. We fought for that, for many years. But you go in there and they won't talk to you. I went in and stood there for half an hour and nobody would even talk to me. And there are so many *people* now. That whole neighborhood is changing. Don't you think so, honey?

DANIEL   Yes!

HOWARD   (*To Gladys, shouting, very loud*)   YES IT'S TOO BAD! IT WAS ONCE A LOVELY NEIGHBORHOOD.

ELLEN   Don't shout please . . .

GLADYS   Oh it was a beautiful neighborhood. We were very happy there. Do you have a lot of friends up in—in the country—up—up in—where you go?

ELLEN   Vermont.

GLADYS   What?

ELLEN   We go to Vermont.

GLADYS   And you have a lot of friends there?

ELLEN   No. Not many. A few.

GLADYS   But the people up there know you? And they come around? Do you entertain much up there?

HOWARD   NO WE DON'T LIKE TO HAVE TOO MANY PEOPLE UP THERE, GLADYS!

ELLEN   Howard don't *shout*, it makes it *worse*.

GLADYS   I didn't hear.

DANIEL   He said—

HOWARD (*Barely lower*)   I SAID, WE GO THERE BECAUSE WE WANT TO GET *AWAY* FROM PEOPLE.

GLADYS   Oh, he's teasing.

HOWARD   NO, WE'RE VERY UNFRIENDLY. WE DON'T LIKE TO SEE TOO MANY PEOPLE.

GLADYS (*To Daniel*)   He's teasing you.

HOWARD   WHEN YOU HAD—LISTEN: WHEN YOU HAD THE HOUSE ON FIRE ISLAND ALL THOSE YEARS, YOU LIKED TO ENTERTAIN ALL THE TIME—

GLADYS   Well sure, everybody likes to have parties—

HOWARD   BUT WE DON'T ENJOY THAT THE WAY YOU DID! WE LOVE THE COUNTRY AND WE LIKE THE SCENERY, BUT WE DON'T LIKE HAVING A LOT OF PEOPLE UP THERE BECAUSE WE SEE TOO MANY PEOPLE HERE IN THE CITY.

GLADYS   Well sure, everybody likes to see people—We used to have people all the time when we went to Fire Island.

HOWARD   RIGHT!

GLADYS   We had a beautiful house there and we entertained quite a lot.

HOWARD   RIGHT! WE DON'T LIKE THAT!

GLADYS   Well it's a beautiful place. (*To Daniel*) Honey, do you want some of these—potatoes?

DANIEL (*Very loud*)   NO THANK YOU.

ELLEN   Danny, you don't have to shout—There she goes.

Gladys is fiddling with her hearing aid.

ELLEN   Don't touch your hearing aid—

GLADYS   It's whistling—

ELLEN (*Getting up*)   Just a minute—Don't touch it—(*She comes around and adjusts the hearing aid.*)

ELLEN Don't hold it with your— all you have to do is— All you have to do is touch it with your finger —Don't grab the knob— Howard, it's too *small* for her, she can't get her finger on it—J—	**GLADYS** There's a terrible whistling. Can you hear that? Does any- body hear that whistling? **HOWARD** Honey, why don't you do it *for* her?

Ellen patiently adjusts the hearing aid.

GLADYS (*Laughs nervously*)   What a crazy business!

HOWARD   Daniel, pass me the potatoes.

Daniel passes the potatoes.

ELLEN (*In a normal voice*)   Can you hear me?

HOWARD (*Takes potatoes*)   Thank you.

Ellen readjusts the hearing aid.

ELLEN (*In a normal voice*)   Can you hear me?

GLADYS   Yes. Perfect. (*She immediately starts to touch the hearing aid.*)

ELLEN	DANIEL
No don't touch it any-more—!	Leave it alone if you can hear!

GLADYS Up! I won't go near it!

They resume eating.

GLADYS You know, Ellen, that one in the gallery, that young artist, has got a sister somewhere who's in a wheelchair, and a mother in—you know, where you go—in the country—

HOWARD NO, GLADYS, WE GO TO VERMONT! HE'S FROM MASSACHUSETTS!

ELLEN	DANIEL
Howard, don't *shout* at her!	You don't have to shout!

GLADYS Oh, he's from Massachusetts? I didn't know that.

ELLEN Yes you did. But you forgot.

GLADYS What?

HOWARD SOMETIMES YOUR MEMORY ISN'T SO GOOD.

GLADYS (*Hearing but ignoring this comment*) Ellen, this dinner is absolutely delicious.

ELLEN Thank you.

GLADYS Absolutely marvelous. (*Pushing a dish of broccoli*) Does anybody want any of this? Honey? Do you want any of this—vegetable? It's very good.

DANIEL No, I've got some of my own right here, thanks!

GLADYS Do you want some?

DANIEL NO I HAVE SOME. THANK YOU!

Gladys offers Daniel some soda.

GLADYS   Would you like some of this drink?

DANIEL   NO THANKS!

ELLEN   Volume.

DANIEL	**GLADYS**
Sorry. Sorry.	It has a very good— flavor. Go ahead and try some. I can't drink all of this.

DANIEL   No thank you.

ELLEN (*Under her breath*)   "Can you cook?"

GLADYS   This dinner is absolutely delicious.

ELLEN   No one could accuse her of being unappreciative.

HOWARD (*To Daniel*)   Are you still seeing that same horrible girl?

GLADYS   Do you know how to cook, honey?

DANIEL (*To Howard*)   Um—I don't really know. I—

GLADYS (*To Daniel*)   Did you ever learn to cook?

DANIEL   A little bit!

Gladys cheers and claps her hands.

GLADYS   You do? Well good for you! Are you a good cook?

HOWARD (*To Daniel*)   Is that not a suitable subject for conversation?

DANIEL (*To Howard*)   Um—(*Turns to Gladys*) I can only cook a little bit! I can't *really* cook—

GLADYS   Well who taught you how?

DANIEL   I taught myself!

HOWARD   Dan? Is that not a suitable subject for conversation?

GLADYS   And do you ever have friends over and—you know—cook 'em up something to eat?

DANIEL (*To Howard*)   No, it doesn't matter. I don't care. She's driving me crazy, that's all.

GLADYS   What's the matter, honey?

DANIEL   Nothing!

HOWARD   Why do you go out with all these crazy girls?

DANIEL   I don't know.

GLADYS   I never learned how to cook. I never used to cook anything.

HOWARD	**GLADYS**
Well as you know, I hate to butt in, but there are several perfectly nice young ladies at the Institute I'd be happy to fix you up with if you're interested—	We had a woman who used to come in and cook for us. . . . Ellen, do you remember Fanny? . . . Ellen? Do you remember Fanny?
DANIEL	**ELLEN** (*Quiet*)
I don't know—I don't really want to—	Yes.
HOWARD	**GLADYS**
Well . . . it's just a	You don't remember her.

22

suggestion . . . It's too
bad you're shy about
that sort of thing.

ELLEN
Of course I remember her.

DANIEL
Yeah, well . . . I . . . I
just . . . I don't know.
I'm not really—

GLADYS
She was a marvelous cook.
She used to cook everything.
I never learned how. I
never liked to cook.

HOWARD   It's fine, sweetheart. Just let me know if you're
interested.

ELLEN   Interested in what?

HOWARD
I offered to fix him up
with one of the young
single women at the
Institute.

GLADYS
Ellen, I want to bring
—that young artist,
the one who's having
a show—the—the one—

ELLEN
Oh . . . !

DANIEL
Don!

HOWARD
There's a very nice young
lady in my program who
mentioned to me that she'd
like to meet somebody,
and I—

GLADYS
Don. Should I ask him
to come up here next
week?

Ellen? You know what
I think I'll do?

ELLEN
Howard—I can't listen
to six different people
talking to me at the same
time—!

Ellen? You know what
I think I'll do?

HOWARD (*To Ellen*)   Sorry.

GLADYS   . . . I'm gonna bring that young artist up with me next week so you can meet him.

ELLEN   Please don't! I don't need anybody new to cook for!

GLADYS   What?

ELLEN   DON'T bring him up next week, I don't want to cook DINNER for everybody! We'll meet him on Saturday. DON'T invite him for dinner!

GLADYS   Don't invite him. Well, that's fine. I don't need to invite him, I don't need to invite anybody. I thought you might want to meet him. He's a very interesting guy.

ELLEN   We will meet him on Saturday.

GLADYS   What?

ELLEN   We will meet him on SATURDAY.

GLADYS   He's from the same place, you know, where you go up—on the weekend—

ELLEN   She's getting worse.

DANIEL   Oh, she's definitely getting worse, Mom.

GLADYS   What's the matter, honey?

DANIEL   Nothing! Everything's fine! Do you want some more?

GLADYS   Oh! No! I couldn't eat another thing.

ELLEN   "You got any coffee lying around?"

GLADYS   Ellen, is there any coffee lying around?

ELLEN Not yet! I'm just about to make some!

GLADYS Does anybody else want any? Honey, do you like coffee?

DANIEL Yes I do.

GLADYS Are you a coffee lover?

DANIEL Yes I am. I'm a coffee lover.

GLADYS Where's the dog?

ELLEN I'm going to blow my brains out.

DANIEL The dog is in the other room!

GLADYS What's the matter? Is she hiding?

DANIEL She's waiting for food.

GLADYS What's the matter? Didn't anybody feed her?

ELLEN No, we're going to let her starve!

HOWARD Honey, please—before we all go insane.

GLADYS Shouldn't somebody give her something?

ELLEN DON'T GIVE HER ANYTHING, SHE'S NOT SUPPOSED TO BEG!

GLADYS Ohhhhhh, the poor thing, she must be hungry.

ELLEN	**DANIEL**
Please don't feed her anything! She's not supposed to beg!	She's fine! She was just fed! She just ate a little while ago!

GLADYS That dog is just the sweetest little animal. Do you take her up with you when you go away to—when you go up to—

DANIEL, HOWARD AND ELLEN Vermont!

GLADYS Is that where it is?

DANIEL (*Getting up*) I have to take a break.

GLADYS Where you going, hon?

DANIEL In the living room!

GLADYS What?

DANIEL (*Leans in, speaks softly*) In the living room.

GLADYS Does anybody want any coffee?

ELLEN I'm just *making* it! Give me five minutes to make it . . . !

DANIEL I'll make it.

Ellen walks out.

GLADYS What's the matter? What's wrong with Ellen?

DANIEL Nothing!

HOWARD She's just tired!

Daniel laughs.

GLADYS Ohhhhhh, poor Ellen. Is she working too hard? I think she works too hard. Your mother works harder than anyone I know. She's always working.

HOWARD Gladys, millions of people work very hard, every day, all day long!

DANIEL What are you trying to do, improve her character?

HOWARD (*Shrugs*) Sure!

GLADYS You got any coffee lyin' around?

DANIEL   I'm just about to make it! (*He goes around the corner to make coffee.*)

GLADYS   You know, I told that young artist that he should get himself . . . should get himself a little—cot, and put it in the back room—

ELLEN (*Off*)   Howard, will you *say* something to her about that?

HOWARD	GLADYS
Honey, what do you want me to say?	—so he won't have to drive all that way every day. He doesn't
ELLEN (*Off*)	know a soul in the
Tell her she can't let him *do* that until we at least *meet* him—	city, and I said, "Well you can't stay with *me,* there's no room in that apartment—"
HOWARD	What's the matter?
Why don't *you* tell her?	

ELLEN (*Off*) Because I've told her five times already—

Daniel reappears, eating ice cream out of the carton.

GLADYS   What's the matter, honey?

DANIEL   Nothing!

GLADYS   This young artist is about the same age as you are— and I think he's very talented. He works like hell on those pictures and he has a very charming personality.

HOWARD   LISTEN: WE WANT TO MEET HIM BEFORE YOU LET HIM MOVE IN THE BACK OF THE GALLERY.

GLADYS   Well you *will* meet him. What's the matter?

HOWARD   BECAUSE, GLADYS—

GLADYS   His mother doesn't live in the city. And I don't think she wants him to be here. I think she's a real nut case.

HOWARD   Gladys—

GLADYS   I think she's kooky.

HOWARD   —GLADYS—LISTEN TO ME.

GLADYS   Yes.

HOWARD   WE DON'T WANT YOU TO AGREE—

ELLEN (*Off*)   Don't *shout*!

HOWARD   Honey, I can't *help* it!

ELLEN (*Off*)   It's too *loud* for her, Howard!

HOWARD (*Slightly lower*)   Gladys, don't tell him he can stay there until we meet him and make sure everything's all right!

GLADYS   I already told him if he wants—

HOWARD   No, Gladys! Listen to me! I'm sure he's very nice, but it's not appropriate to have him stay there until we make sure there's nothing peculiar about him.

GLADYS   Well why should he have to lug that car around when nobody's in that room all day long—

HOWARD (*On "nobody's"*)   It's not appropriate to have a stranger sleeping in the back of the gallery if you don't know anything about him.

GLADYS   But he's not living with *me*. *I* don't want that, I'm not lookin' for that anymore . . . !

HOWARD   I understand that. And I'm also sure he's perfectly harmless. But until we meet him, you still have to tell him he's going to have to make some other arrangement.

ELLEN (*Off*)   How is she going to do that? She can't even remember his *name*.

HOWARD	**GLADYS**
Then *you* tell her, because	What's the matter?
I—(*To Gladys*) Nothing!	What's wrong?
Just do what you're told.	
You know how to do that.	

GLADYS   I always do what I'm told!

HOWARD   Right! Except when you don't want to!

GLADYS   Well what's wrong with that?

Everyone laughs.

HOWARD   Just wait until we meet him! And don't argue!

GLADYS   All right, who's arguing?

DANIEL (*Eating ice cream*)   Mom, do you want any ice cream?

ELLEN (*Off*)   No thank you.

DANIEL   Well, I'm going to finish it . . .

ELLEN (*Off*)   Be my guest.

Gladys hums to herself because no one is talking to her.

HOWARD   Is this girl you're seeing also involved in politics?

DANIEL   I'm not actually seeing her, she can't make up her mind whether or not I'm seeing her . . .

HOWARD   Is she involved in politics?

DANIEL   No, she's involved in torture. She comes over and she tortures me and then she goes away and looks around for somebody to torture her—which she actually seems to prefer—but she has extremely high standards, so if she can't find anyone sufficiently diabolical, she comes back and tortures me some more.

HOWARD   Jesus Christ. She sounds delightful.

DANIEL   Oh, she's great.

Ellen enters and goes over to Gladys.

ELLEN (*Softly*)   Why don't you go sit in the living room and I'll bring you some coffee?

GLADYS   Ellen? Can I do something in here? Do you want me to do the dishes?

ELLEN   No thanks. There's nothing to do.

Gladys hums to herself again under the following:

DANIEL   Anyway, it doesn't matter because she's going to Turkey next week anyway.

ELLEN   Turkey! What's she doing in Turkey?

DANIEL   I don't know. Traveling around. Lecturing at a torture symposium, I don't know.

ELLEN	**HOWARD**
Well, maybe she'll stay there!	Good! Maybe she'll emigrate!

GLADYS   Ellen, can I help clean off the table?

ELLEN   No thank you. It's almost done. (*Ellen goes around the corner.*)

HOWARD   Is this girl in analysis?

DANIEL   Yes. Unfortunately her analyst recently committed suicide.

HOWARD   He did? No . . .

DANIEL   Yes. That's the third psychoanalyst who's tried to treat her and ended up killing himself. She's cutting a swath of terror through the New York Psychoanalytic Institute. I'm surprised you guys haven't seen anything about it in the *Psychoanalytic Quarterly*.

HOWARD (*Laughing*)   Come on . . . !

DANIEL (*Laughing*)   It's true—They say she has no superego. They're dropping like flies.

They laugh. Gladys smiles.

GLADYS   What's he laughing at, honey? What's he laughing at? What's everybody laughing at?

DANIEL   Nothing, nothing, it's not important.

He starts reading a section of the newspaper. Howard eats a cookie. Gladys resumes humming to herself.

The gallery. Howard is talking to Don. Daniel is looking at the pictures.

DON   Oh yeah, she's a terrific lady. Only I don't think that hearing aid of hers is very powerful because I often have to repeat myself when I'm talkin' to her. But she is extremely sharp. You can see that right away—

HOWARD   Yes she is, in her own inimitable fashion—

DON   But I can see where it's already kind of frustrating—because you know, like, the other day: I was movin' my car—That's my car right out front there—the maroon one, the Lincoln—and when I come back, Gladys says to me there was a couple in here and they want to buy a picture . . . !

HOWARD   Oh—!

DON   So I'm thinkin', "Terrific!" I been in New York City two weeks, I got my pictures up in a gallery in Greenwich Village, and I just sold my first picture!

HOWARD   Congratulations!

DON   Wait—that's not the end of it. Because it turns out she didn't get a *name*.

HOWARD (*Smiles to Daniel*)   Jesus Christ . . .

DON   I *think,* because she couldn't *hear* them. And I almost tear the place apart lookin' for a scrap of paper or something in case she wrote it down, and don't you know it: No name, no paper, and I'm still waitin' for 'em. They sure haven't been back yet.

HOWARD   I'm afraid that's more her memory than her hearing aid . . .

DON   Well, she remembers stuff, but plenty of times I'll say something to her and I can tell, kinda *tell* she didn't really hear me, but she doesn't want to let on. So I think it's the hearing aid problem more than anything else . . . They make some pretty good ones now. I don't know what kind she's got now, but boy, it'd be great if somebody could get her a better one. Because God only knows how many pictures I really sold, if you see what I mean. But I'm not complaining. She's a great lady, but she's just kinda stubborn.

Ellen comes in from the street.

HOWARD   Yes she is. (*To Ellen*) Hello there.

ELLEN   Hello. (*She sits*) Blurf. What a day.

DON   Everything all right?

ELLEN   Oh, fine. Howard, I made her show me how she does her insulin, and she's been—she sticks the needle *through* the gauze pad, and then she pulls plunger *up*—so all she does is fill the syringe with blood, and then she throws it away. So—

HOWARD	**DANIEL**
For Christ's sake . . .	I'm amazed she can even *see* that needle.

ELLEN   —for all I know she hasn't taken it for *days*. *Weeks,* for all I know.

HOWARD   Well, maybe we should—

ELLEN   I'm going to have Florence do it when she comes in the mornings, but she's only there twice a week. We're gonna have to get someone to come in the rest of the time. It doesn't seem to be *killing* her, but . . .

DON   What's wrong, she has diabetes?

ELLEN   Yes, very mild—she takes *this* much insulin in the mornings. (*Indicates tiny amount*) But you still have to do it every day. I'm gonna talk to Dr Wagner again . . . (*Pause*) That *sign* of hers outside is really crummy looking. It's half *off*. I'm gonna call my cousin Bill.

DANIEL   Hey, did you see the renovations they're doing in the hotel?

HOWARD   Oh yes . . .

ELLEN   Yes, he's really jazzing it up. I looked inside. They've got a new floor and an iron—gate—or trellis or something. It actually looks rather nice.

DANIEL   Yeah, the whole lobby was like *rubble* for about six months, but now it looks pretty good—

HOWARD (*To Don*)   The hotel this gallery is a part of used to be the seediest, most God-awful place—

ELLEN   That's not true. When I was growing up it was very nice. It was a nice, rather quaint, residential Greenwich Village hotel . . .

DON   Is there somethin' wrong with the guy who runs it? Gladys . . .

ELLEN   Oh—

HOWARD   No, that's just—

ELLEN   —He snubbed her, or she thinks he snubbed her, or maybe he said hello and she didn't *hear* him . . . I don't know. Anyway . . .

HOWARD Anyway, that was *it. Criminal.*

ELLEN Well *I* don't know. Maybe he *was* rude to her. I think he's a little peculiar.

DON Yeah, I met that guy, the owner—Mr. Georgio? Georgianni?

ELLEN George. Alan George.

DON I thought he was Italian.

ELLEN I don't think so . . .

DON "Georgio." That sounds Italian.

ELLEN	**DANIEL**
. . . unless he changed his name or something.	I thought he was Jewish. He's Jewish, that guy.

HOWARD They probably changed it at Ellis Island, like everyone else. Right?

DON Are you all Jewish?

(*Pause.*)

ELLEN	**DANIEL**
Well—yes . . .	I'm half-Jewish. But since my mother's
HOWARD (*To Daniel*) You're Jewish. You're Jewish. You're *Jewish.*	Jewish, that means I'm Jewish—by ancient Jewish law.

ELLEN We're not very religious.

HOWARD What do you mean we're not very religious? We're not religious at *all.* Except *I* was raised—

DANIEL We're liberal Upper West Side atheistic Jewish intellectuals—and we really like German choral music.

Ellen and Howard laugh.

DON   My family's not very religious either. Well, I suppose my father was, in a way, but not really . . . He used to drag me kickin' and screamin' to church every Sunday, but my mother always stayed at home . . .

Silence.

HOWARD   Actually, it's very interesting: Gladys' father was from Russia, where he was a bookmaker for the Czar—

ELLEN	**DANIEL**
Book*binder,* Howard. He wasn't—	He was a book*binder*. It wasn't like he was the Czar's *bookie*.

HOWARD   Yes, excuse me, bookbinder for the Czar. And he came here in the teens, I think, or possibly earlier—

ELLEN   Oh, I think earlier, Howard—

HOWARD   And he founded a very successful publishing business by carting Jewish religious books around the Lower East Side in a wheelbarrow—

DON   Really.

HOWARD   Until Gladys' nephew took it over from *his* father and proceeded to run it into the ground. Right? Schmuck!

DON   No, I didn't know that—

ELLEN	**HOWARD**
And my mother—	And Gladys thinks it's all bullshit.

ELLEN   Yes, my whole childhood I was raised to think that anybody who was religious *at all* was some kind of *moron*.

HOWARD   Gladys is very broad-minded.

ELLEN   Well, she was always—

HOWARD   Right? Like a good communist.

ELLEN   Well, she *was* a communist. I spent my whole childhood listening to her and my father and their friends argue *politics* all night long. My father would sit there and play devil's advocate to all my mother's friends, they'd have screaming fights until two in the morning and then she'd get up at the crack of dawn to go stand on a milk carton in Washington Square and campaign for low-income housing. She was very impressive in her own maddening way. But those discussions used to drive me *crazy* . . .

HOWARD   Really? I always thought you enjoyed them . . .

ELLEN   Ha ha.

HOWARD (*To Don*)   But I'll tell you, if you ever wanted anything done in New York, you called Gladys.

ELLEN   Oh yes.

DANIEL   Oh yeah.

HOWARD   An apartment, a *job,* a lawyer . . .

ELLEN   A moving company—Remember she used to hire those crazy Israeli movers . . . ?

DANIEL   I remember them.

ELLEN   One of them was a *sculptor* and one was a *musician* . . .

DANIEL   Yeah. Mom, they were both *insane.*

HOWARD (*Simultaneous, to Don*)   When I was divorced from my first wife, I called Gladys and I told her I needed an apartment, and in *twenty-four hours* she found me a wonderful little apartment on Eighty-sixth Street, right across the park from where my children were living, with a separate office space so I could see patients—and half a block from the park so I could walk my dog.

DON   Really.

HOWARD   . . . It was amazing!

ELLEN (*To Howard & Don*)   She was very good at that . . .

DANIEL (*To Don*)   When I was a little kid she was always going off on these trips around the world—She took me to the Yucatán when I was ten so I could see the pyramids—

HOWARD   . . . And by the time she got off the boat she'd know everybody on board, she'd know everything about them . . .

ELLEN   Right, and then she'd bring them all back to New York and invite them over so I could cook dinner for them.

HOWARD (*To Ellen*)   A lot's changed in twenty years, kid!

ELLEN   And then she'd take *Zique* with her. (*Pronounced like "Zeke"*)

DANIEL   She used to have this psychotic Dalmatian—

ELLEN   Zique!

HOWARD   Which is spelled—

ELLEN
Z-I-Q-U-E, for   **HOWARD** (*on Ellen's "Q"*)
some reason.   Z-I-Q-U-E

DANIEL   —who used to hide under the table when anybody came into the room.

ELLEN   And who she used to take on these cruises where they didn't allow dogs—

DANIEL   And she'd say—

ELLEN   "Oh, they don't allow dogs on that boat but I just take her anyway—"

DANIEL & ELLEN   "—*They* don't mind."

HOWARD (*To Don*)   This was the craziest fuckin' dog you ever met.

ELLEN (*To Howard*)   Right, because *you* told her to get her.

HOWARD   I didn't tell her to get *Zique*.

ELLEN	**DANIEL**
You did too!	Yes you did!

HOWARD (*To Don*)   I told Gladys I thought she should get a *dog*—

ELLEN   Boy, was she mad at you.

HOWARD   —because at the time, we were worried about her being in the gallery by herself with all the crazies running around . . .

DANIEL   The worst thing that's gonna happen to her in this neighborhood is that somebody's gonna try to sell her *pot*.

ELLEN (*To Howard*)   Right, and she got very offended . . .

HOWARD   Right, she got very offended . . .

ELLEN   . . . because you called her a little old lady . . .

HOWARD   Because I told her I didn't think it was such a great idea for a little old lady to sit by herself in the window all day long, when you've got—

ELLEN   And was she mad!

HOWARD   What can I say? I was my usual tactful self.

ELLEN   . . . And this was fifteen *years* ago.

DANIEL   Yeah, so you said she should get an *attack* dog.

HOWARD   I didn't say an *attack* dog. Come on!

ELLEN	**DANIEL**
Yes you did, Howard.	Yes you did! You said she should get a German shepherd!

HOWARD (*To Daniel, on "German"*)   I told her to get a *dog,* in case some lunatic walks in, she should have a dog who's gonna bark at them and scare them away. (*To Don*) Right? So she goes to the pound—

DANIEL (*To Don*)	**HOWARD**
And she comes back with—	—and she comes back with this skinny little cadaverous Dalmatian—

DANIEL   Who *shakes*!

HOWARD   —who *shakes*, and hides under the table every time you come into the room!

Ellen, Daniel and Howard are all laughing.

DON   That's funny . . .

HOWARD   . . . so I said, "Gladys, what the hell are you *doing*? That dog wouldn't scare *any*body!"

ELLEN   . . . She was very fond of her.

HOWARD   Listen, it was a wonderful thing for her.

ELLEN   Zique wasn't so bad. She just shook.

DANIEL   Unbelievable.

Silence.

HOWARD (*To Don*)   Well . . . you don't seem too dangerous.

DON   Oh . . . Thank you.

Pause.

HOWARD	DON
So—	Now all you gotta do is tell that to Mr Georgio.

ELLEN   Oh no don't worry about him. I don't think he ever comes *in* here.

DON   Oh, he was sure in here the other *day*. And I don't think he was too happy about my bein' here . . .

Pause. Ellen and Howard look at each other and then back at Don.

ELLEN   Oh really?

HOWARD   Really?

Pause. Don is a bit taken aback.

DON   Well, yeah—

DANIEL	ELLEN
Why? What did he say?	Did he say anything to you?

DON   Oh no, he just—

ELLEN   I didn't think he ever came *in* here . . .

DON   No, he's been in here a couple of times. He—

ELLEN   My mother always thought he was rather strange.

HOWARD   What did he say?

DON   I don't remember exactly. I didn't talk to him for very long . . .

ELLEN   Well, I don't see why he should mind . . .

DANIEL   Yeah, what does he care?

HOWARD   Listen: He's probably just being a pain in the ass.

DON   Oh, I think he's probably worried somebody's gonna see me in here late at night and think I'm tryin' to rob the place.

DANIEL   Rob it of what?

HOWARD   No—That's crazy.

DANIEL   What would you steal?

DON   No, I could see his point. Somebody could come in at night and try to steal my pictures off the walls.

Pause.

DANIEL   What do mean, like, Art Thieves?

HOWARD   No . . .

DON   It could happen.

DANIEL   I don't think so.

HOWARD   It's highly unlikely.

ELLEN   I'll give him a call on Monday. But I don't see why he should have any objection—

DON   Yeah, he probably had a bee in his bonnet about something else . . . He said he was gonna talk to Gladys, so he probably straightened it out with her.

DANIEL (*A joke:*)   Oh yes. I'm sure she cleared everything right up.

HOWARD   At any rate, I don't think we have to worry about that now . . .

ELLEN   I'll give him a call . . . I hope that's not going to be a problem.

HOWARD   I don't think so, honey. (*To Don*) Listen: I think we'd like to buy one of your pictures.

DON   Oh—! That's great. Wow. That's—OK, fantastic.

HOWARD   My oldest son is having a birthday next week, and his wife is expecting a baby, and I think one of these would make a terrific birthday gift.

DON   Great. Uh—

HOWARD (*Pointing*)   I like this one. Do you like this one, sweetheart?

ELLEN (*Looking*)   Ooh, yes.

DON   Oh yeah, that's a little wharf in my home town. I tried really hard to get in all the details. This guy here runs a bait and tackle store. And these birds—the birds come and sit on top of this guy's sign all day long. Drives him nuts, 'cause— well, you know, 'cause they deface the sign. So he's always out there cleaning it off. I didn't put that in. I tried to be faithful to what's actually there, otherwise . . .

HOWARD
Sold. Sold. Now, I notice
you don't have any prices   **DON**
on these . . . How about . . .   Oh, well, I, uh . . .
Is three hundred dollars . . .
fair?

DON (*Disappointed*)   Oh. Sure. Absolutely. That's great . . .
You know, you're Gladys' family . . . Three hundred—
that's more than fair. That's one of my favorites. And
that's—a nice—uh—frame you're getting, too—

HOWARD   And listen: You don't have to worry about Gladys
forgetting our names! Right?

DON   Right. Right.

ELLEN (*Cheerfully*)   I remember when she *got* this place.

ACT ONE, SCENE FIVE

As Daniel comes forward and addresses the audience, Ellen's kitchen lights up. Ellen talks on the phone silently, slowly turning her back to us.

DANIEL (*To the audience*)   My mother called Mr. George, who said he had no problem with Don staying in the gallery. So Don moved into the little room in the back—which was basically a closet—he moved his car around, he walked my grandmother back and forth from the house, and sometimes he cooked her lunch. Late at night if you looked past the drug dealers on the corner, you could usually see Don through the gallery window, hovering over his pictures, touching them up with a little brush.

My mother hired a nurse's aide named Marva to come in the mornings when Florence wasn't there, to give Gladys breakfast and help with her insulin. She hated it. She said there were these *women* in the house and they wouldn't go away. Mom took her to the eye doctor and the ear doctor. Paid her bills, paid her taxes. I dropped by her apartment to say hello once in a while. I let her take me to dinner once a month at the restaurant next door. They were really nice to her there, so she really liked that. She rang my doorbell, a *lot*. Sometimes I was nice to her. Sometimes I yelled at her. And she went to the gallery, almost every day. Until winter came and she stopped going to the gallery for the time being because she couldn't stand the cold. So she stayed in her apartment with those *women* and we waited for the spring.

Then in January, Mr. George called my mother and told her he was taking away the gallery and turning it into a breakfast cafe for his hotel.

Daniel turns and enters the kitchen.

ELLEN   Anyway—

DANIEL   What did he say?

ELLEN   He says he's turning the gallery into a cafe and connecting it to the rest of the hotel, and he wants her to be out by the end of May.

DANIEL   The end of *May*? He's got to be kidding.

ELLEN   I *knew* something like this would happen . . .

DANIEL   Well can't he—I mean, can't we—Can he *do* that? Doesn't he have to—

ELLEN   Well, honey, she doesn't even have a lease.

DANIEL   She doesn't have a *lease*?

ELLEN   No, she always said she—

DANIEL   She's been in there for twenty-eight years and she doesn't have a lease?

ELLEN   No. And you know, I asked him if it was because Don's been in there for so long and he said, "Oh no, it's got nothing to do with that." But maybe he thinks she's peculiar, sitting there all day long . . . And then Don's in there at night . . . I don't know, maybe it's no good for his new . . . I don't really know. He obviously has—he's having plans drawn up, so . . . (*Pause*) It's just—if he kicks her out I don't know what she's going to *do*.

Pause.

DANIEL   How can she not have a lease?

ELLEN   I don't know. She used to say she didn't want a lease because then he could raise the rent.

DANIEL   What?

ELLEN   I don't *know*. Nobody ever used that space. It's not even attached to the rest of the hotel. But he wants to knock a wall down and put in a kitchen and use it as a breakfast cafe for the hotel.

DANIEL   Well, can't she . . . (*Pause*) I mean, what if we say no? What can he—

ELLEN   Well I thought of that, honey, but if she has no lease there's really not much we can do about it. We could refuse to get out, but then he could start sending in process servers and people to harass her and I don't want that . . .

DANIEL   No . . .

ELLEN   . . . She wouldn't know what was going on.

DANIEL   Serve somebody right if he sent them in there after her—they'd run out screaming.

ELLEN (*Short laugh*)   Right.

GLADYS (*Off*)   Ellen? Ellen?

DANIEL   What is she gonna *do*?

ELLEN   I don't know.

GLADYS (*Off*)   Hello? Hello? Ellen? Where are you? Where'd you go?

Ellen goes out.

ELLEN (*Off*) I'm just in the kitchen! I'm just ta—I'm just talking to Danny about something!	**GLADYS** (*Off*) Where were you, honey? What's the matter?

GLADYS (*Off*)   What's the matter? Is he crying?

DANIEL (*To himself*) Am I what?

ELLEN (*Off*) No! Why would he be crying?

GLADYS (*Off*) I don't know. I thought somebody was crying.

ELLEN (*Off*) You were probably having a dream! Why don't you sit here and in a few minutes I'll bring you something to drink!

GLADYS (*Off*) All right. I'll stay here.

Ellen enters.

ELLEN You don't look like you're crying.

DANIEL Mom, this is really bad.

ELLEN Well, I can ask Arthur if he knows some kind of fancy legal maneuver, but I'm pretty sure there's nothing to be done.

DANIEL Yeah, because maybe—Don't they have to give notice, or something?

ELLEN He's giving us five months.

DANIEL Five months.

ELLEN She doesn't even go there in the winter. I don't think she's been in there since November. She just sits all day long in that tiny little apartment. *You're* busy, and I can't have her up here more than once or twice a week or I go out of my mind. She complained to me all last winter how she's lonely, she's lonely—well she *is* very lonely. She won't *read*—or she *can't* read—And Florence, who's a *saint,* says she can't even figure out how to work the television . . . What's she going to *do* all day long? (*Pause*) And I feel bad for *you.* I only get it twice a week, but you're on the front lines—

DANIEL Listen—I'm not—

ELLEN You can't spend your life running around taking care of her. Karl says he went in yesterday and she was asleep on the sofa . . .

DANIEL Yeah I know, you told me.

ELLEN And she had left the coffee pot lying on its side on the burner and the entire apartment was filled with smoke.

DANIEL I know. You *told* me.

ELLEN I'm afraid one of these days she's going to burn the whole house down.

Silence.

ELLEN He's got some fuckin' nerve kicking her out of that gallery for his—fuckin' hotel expansions.

DANIEL I know . . .

Pause.

ELLEN I mean, eventually she's going to have to move in here, but I'm dreading that day. Because when she does, *I'm* going to have to move *out*.

DANIEL Well—

ELLEN (*Her voice suddenly catches*) Do you know what she said to me last week? (*Pause*) She wants to get a job in a *law* firm. Did I know anybody who she could work for as a *lawyer*. (*Pause*) And now Don's on her shit list because he wants to visit his mother again—

DANIEL Yeah I know, she gave me a whole long monologue about that recently—

Ellen sees something and walks out.

ELLEN (*Off*) PLEASE DON'T FEED THE DOG!

GLADYS (*Off*) But she's so hungry—!

ELLEN (*Off*) I'M GOING TO FEED HER *DINNER* IN A FEW MINUTES! DON'T *FEED* HER, SHE'S NOT SUPPOSED TO BEG!

GLADYS (*Off*) Well what are you so angry about?

DANIEL Mom . . . !

Ellen stalks in with a plate of crackers and cheese. She clatters it down on the table.

ELLEN Howard thinks we should get her a cat.

DANIEL A cat?

ELLEN Well, you don't have to walk a cat, and you can leave its food out all day long, and it shits in a cat box, and she's so fond of Daisy, so maybe it's not such a terrible idea. She can feed it all day long until it explodes. She'll love it.

DANIEL Yeah, but what happens if she opens her door at night and it runs out? How's she gonna get it back?

ELLEN I don't know . . . That's probably a good point. (*Looks offstage*) Here she comes . . . I'm not going to tell her now.

DANIEL No . . .

ELLEN I'm not up to it . . .

DANIEL Well, we can wait a little while till we figure out what to do.

Gladys enters.

GLADYS   What's the matter, Ellen? Ellen? What's the matter?

ELLEN (*Loud but not too loud*)   I really wish you wouldn't feed the dog scraps. We don't want her to beg.

GLADYS   I want to talk to you about that young—artist—you know—he wants to put up a show—

ELLEN   No he *is* putting up a show.

GLADYS	
But now he says he's leaving! He's going back to—to where he lives, and he's leaving me all his pictures! He says he's just packing off and leaving them there! And—	**ELLEN** What? . . . No he's not. No he's not.
	DANIEL He's just going—
	ELLEN He's not leaving. Stop talking a minute. Stop talking.

GLADYS   I never know where he *is*! One day he shows up, one day he's going *away*—I never—

ELLEN   *Listen* to me! He is just going home for the weekend! He will be back on Monday!

GLADYS   Who told you that?

DANIEL & ELLEN   HE DID!

Gladys winces in pain and touches her hearing aid.

GLADYS   What?

DANIEL   *He* did.

ELLEN   He has to go home for a few days to see his mother and to make a little money. He's not leaving you the pictures. He's only going for the weekend.

GLADYS   No.

DANIEL
Yes! He's going home to make some money and to see his mother . . . He wants to see his mother!

ELLEN (*To Daniel*)
What are we gonna tell *him*?

GLADYS   Well what's she buggin' him for? *I* can't put up that show myself! I don't know what to do!

DANIEL   You don't have to do anything! He's going to be back in THREE DAYS!

GLADYS   Three days? Why didn't he tell me that?

ELLEN   He did tell you. You just forgot.

GLADYS   I think he's very sneaky.

DANIEL   Fine. He's sneaky. But he'll be back in three days.

ELLEN (*To Daniel*)   I'm going to call Arthur. Although I'm sure he'll say there's nothing to be done—

Offstage the front door opens.

GLADYS   Has anybody fed the dog?

ELLEN   —but I might as well—

Howard comes in, in a suit, carrying a soft briefcase.

HOWARD   Hello, dear. (*Kisses Daniel*) How are you?

DANIEL   Hi.

GLADYS   Hello!

HOWARD (*Kisses Gladys*)   HELLO, GLADYS!

He crosses away from Gladys and kisses Ellen.

HOWARD   Hello, dear.

ELLEN   Mr. George is taking back the gallery.

HOWARD   He's what?

ELLEN   He's building a cafe for the hotel and he wants her to be out in May.

HOWARD   Oh, fuck.

GLADYS   Did anybody feed the dog?

HOWARD   Have you told her?

ELLEN   No, I have to get up my nerve. And I also think I should call Arthur and see what he thinks—

HOWARD   Oh, *shit*.

GLADYS (*To Daniel*)   Honey?

DANIEL (*Trying to listen to Howard and Ellen*)   Just a minute . . . !

ELLEN	**GLADYS**
Although I'm fairly sure there's nothing she can do about it. She doesn't have a lease, I don't think there's anything written down, and he wants to put in the cafe *this summer*.	Did anybody give the dog her supper? **DANIEL** Not yet. We'll feed her in a few minutes! **GLADYS** What?

HOWARD
When did he call?

DANIEL
We'll feed her in a
few minutes!

ELLEN
Ten minutes ago.

GLADYS   Do you think the Village has changed lately?

DANIEL   Yes!

GLADYS (*Applauds*)   Well! Somebody agrees with me!

DANIEL   Uh-huh!

HOWARD
All right. Why don't
you go call Arthur?

GLADYS
I sit in that window all
day long, and it never used
to be so crowded before.

ELLEN
I don't even know if he's
still in the office. He's
probably gone by now.

DANIEL (*To Gladys*)
Uh-huh!

HOWARD   Why don't you call him anyway? Call him at
home.

ELLEN   Well, I don't want to bother him at home. I can—

HOWARD   Honey—!

DANIEL   Mom, for Christ's sake, call him at home! He won't
mind.

HOWARD   Your mother is very pushy.

GLADYS   What's the matter, honey?

DANIEL   Nothing!

54

ELLEN Maybe he's still at the office. (*She exits.*)

GLADYS Where's Ellen going?

DANIEL Nowhere!

GLADYS The man who runs that hotel is changing the whole place. I saw him on the street, and his daughter was looking for him and he walked right by her and he wouldn't even talk to her! She was crying. She was. And he's got a lot of people from Europe in there now.

DANIEL Uh-huh!

HOWARD Dan, I was thinking that she likes Daisy so much, it might be a nice thing for her if we got her a little cat.

GLADYS (*To Daniel*) Honey, do you know how to cook?

DANIEL (*Trying to answer Howard*) A little!

GLADYS Your mother is a wonderful cook. I never learned how to cook anything!

HOWARD Dan . . . ?

DANIEL
Yeah, I know, but I told Mom I don't know what she's going to do if she opens the door and it runs out. She couldn't get it back, she can't chase it up the stairs, or if it gets out on the street—(*To Gladys*) Yes!

GLADYS
Are you still writing for the newspaper, honey?

Honey? Are you still writing for that newspaper?

GLADYS Are you working hard?

DANIEL   So-so!

GLADYS   So-so. Well that's good.

HOWARD   Well—it's just a thought. Maybe we could put up a gate . . .

Ellen enters. During the following, Gladys hums to herself.

ELLEN   He's not there. I left him a—

DANIEL   Did you call him at home?

ELLEN   No, I left a message for him at the office. I don't want to bother him at home—

HOWARD   Honey, for Christ's sake . . . !

ELLEN   I will call him in the morning! They're not kicking her out *tomorrow*!

GLADYS   Kicking who out?

They turn to her, startled that she heard this.

Silence.

ELLEN   Nobody. We're talking about somebody you don't know.

GLADYS   Oh.

Gladys resumes humming.

ELLEN   I don't know what to tell her. We're going to have to move her in here and then I'm going to slit my wrists.

Gladys spots the dog, offstage.

GLADYS   Look at the dog. She's crying.

DANIEL   No she's not!

GLADYS   She wants to come in here. Nobody's talking to her.

Pause.

ELLEN   I'm going to start dinner.

Ellen exits.

ACT TWO, SCENE ONE

Ellen's living room. Gladys sits. Ellen stands nearby. Daniel stands downstage, holding an unopened bottle of beer. He addresses the audience.

DANIEL   Now came the time to tell Gladys they were taking away her gallery. We avoided it for as long as we could because we had no idea what to do with her afterwards. She was starting to lose some words. She couldn't really remember anybody's name except Ellen's, and she didn't recognize anyone outside the immediate family anymore. My father came to New York for a visit and she knew she was glad to see him, but she didn't quite know who he was. Long monologues that used to be part of her regular repertoire dropped out of her conversation for good. I stopped going out to dinner with her because it got to be too much of an ordeal. She rang my doorbell so much I stopped answering it all the time. Instead I'd just go to the door and look through the peephole to make sure she was OK, and then I'd watch this weird little convex image of her turn around in the hallway and go back into her apartment.

Every day I came home from work, knowing she'd been alone all afternoon, and I listened at her door, hoping she'd be asleep so I wouldn't have to go in, knowing that if I didn't, she'd be alone all night until Marva showed up in the morning.

But as soon as it got warmer she started going to the gallery again. She sat there and talked to Don and anybody else who wandered in, and it really seemed to cheer her up. One time she got hysterical about something when she was alone in the gallery, and the cops came by and this one young cop told me, "She shouldn't be left alone like that: It's not safe." Sometimes people talked as if we weren't facing the true degree of her decline—and maybe we weren't. But I don't know what we were supposed to do. She didn't want to live with Mom any more than Mom wanted to live with her. Mom never even talked about putting her in a nursing home. She just didn't want to do that. And I thought it was better for her to be at risk alone in the gallery than to be locked in her apartment all day long.

He opens the beer and goes into the living room to join Ellen and Gladys. (NOTE: While Gladys now has a lot of trouble finding the right words, she still knows exactly what she is trying to say, and still addresses herself directly to the others with the same dogged persistence. In other words, she is not lost in her own world, nor disconnected from the others, nor is she talking to herself. She at all times pressures them for answers, and when they ignore or placate her it drives her even harder to get a real response from them.)

GLADYS I want to sell that—there are two—places, and I want to sell one of them, and find another place. Because I can't stay there all day long, and there's a woman there who comes in every day. She's a very good-looking black woman, and I went to the bathroom and she was standing there, standing up, peeing like a man, into the—*cup.*

ELLEN Have you heard this one yet?

DANIEL Yeah, you told me.

GLADYS She was making a pass! And she wouldn't go away! Just *looking* at me! With the door wide open. And the one in the gallery, I told him to go around to the—places, on

Madison Avenue, and go in and bring them an—invi—
invitation, because he's opening a show—

ELLEN   All right. I'm going to tell her.

DANIEL   All right.

GLADYS   Those pictures have been up for a few weeks now
and he hasn't even had the show yet, and I said to him—

ELLEN   LISTEN: MR. GEORGE IS TAKING AWAY THE
GALLERY. HE WANTS TO TAKE THE GALLERY
BACK FOR THE HOTEL, SO YOU'RE GOING TO
HAVE TO MOVE OUT OF THE GALLERY IN TWO
MONTHS, AFTER DON OPENS HIS SHOW.

Pause.

GLADYS   Well *good* then. I'll give it up and that'll be that for
that, and I'll get a job being a lawyer.

ELLEN   You don't have to worry about that right now. You
have another two months before you have to move out,
and there's plenty—

GLADYS   Because I can't run that place by myself! So I'll sell
it and get myself set up in an—an—a house—an office. (*To
Daniel*) Maybe you can take that place in the front for me,
honey, and you can use it for the newspaper.

DANIEL   No, I don't need another place, that's your
apartment. You don't have to move out of your apartment,
only the gallery!

GLADYS   As soon as my—foot—gets better, I'm gonna start
lookin' around for a town—so I can move to another town.

ELLEN   Jesus Christ, she's really—it's word salad.

GLADYS   Because I can't manage by myself! And there's one woman who comes in and sits there—Hm! (*She demonstrates*) And she doesn't say a word all day long. And I want someone to get *rid* of her.

ELLEN   We can't get rid of her—

GLADYS   They want me to cook for them, and throw a party, and entertain them, but I can't *do* that anymore. I'm sick!

ELLEN   They're there to cook for *you*! They are helping me take care of you, because otherwise I have to come down every day and do your insulin myself. They are there to make things easier for *me*.

GLADYS   Well they *should* help you! You have your own family—

ELLEN   We can talk about that later. I just wanted to tell you that Mr. George is taking back the gallery, but we don't have to do anything for a couple of months!

GLADYS   Well who's gonna take care of all those pictures? I'll have to talk with that man, I know his daughter—

ELLEN   Don will take care of the pictures, he'll take the pictures with him.

GLADYS   Well—I've had that—the—the place—

ELLEN   Gallery.

GLADYS   —gallery, for many years and nobody comes in there. So I'll sell it. You can have the place in the front, and I'll get a job in an office. (*To Daniel*) Do they have any jobs in your office, honey?

Silence.

62

ELLEN   We can talk about that later. You'll have one last opening with Don's show, and we can worry about your apartment later.

GLADYS   I think that's very sensible. Worry about it later. Good!

Daniel and Ellen look at each other—i.e., it can't be this easy.

ACT TWO, SCENE TWO

The gallery. Don's opening. On the desk is a big platter of cheese and crackers, plastic cups and paper napkins and a bottle of wine. Gladys sits behind the desk. Don and Daniel stand together, across the room from her; each has a plastic cup of wine. Don is eating cheese. Everyone is in a good mood, especially Gladys and Don.

DON   But every time I try to tell her I'm just goin' back home for a few days to see my mother, she goes haywire. It's that darn hearing aid.

DANIEL   You've got to be kidding. It's not her hearing aid.

DON   No, I'm tellin' you, it's not a good model. And this stuff about my mother is just plain ridiculous.

DANIEL   Yeah, well, it's been really great that you've been in here, it's been great for her—

GLADYS   Your mother was here before, sweet. I don't know what happened to her. Is she coming down?

DANIEL   She went to do some errands. She'll be back later.

GLADYS	DON
She came in and then she just went—she—I don't know what happened to her. Do you want some of this—bottle—some of this—Do you want some of this— liquor?	Yeah, she was in before with your step-father. They came in a few hours ago—
	DANIEL
	Yeah, I know, I saw them at the house. (*To Gladys*) No thank you! I have some!

DON Well, I'm really excited. I put an ad in this art news letter newspaper. I been bustin' my back on these pictures, and I don't mind tellin' you I'm pretty excited. You know, I think the problem before was that I didn't really have an "opening." People would look in, but I was workin' on the pictures—

GLADYS So what's new, honey? Are you working hard? Is everything kablooey in the back of the—

DANIEL No, everything's fine!

DON You know—I was workin' on the pictures literally day and night, and then with the cold weather she didn't come in too much, but now it's all set and the weather's good. I don't know if you noticed the new sign—

DANIEL Yeah, my cousin Bill made it: He put it up in the winter, didn't he?

DON	**GLADYS**
Oh yeah, yeah, right. You been in since then, haven't you?	I want to sell that place in the—the business in the— When my—toe—
DANIEL	I want to get rid
Yeah, a lot. I was here when the cops came . . .	of that place, it's too dark for me in the winter. And now
DON	there's a little
Yeah, what the heck was that all about?	*girl*—

DANIEL I don't know. She thought somebody was—(*To Gladys*) What?

GLADYS   What's the matter, honey?

DANIEL   NOTHING. I DIDN'T HEAR WHAT YOU SAID.

GLADYS   What did I say?

DANIEL   I don't know.

GLADYS   Well, me neither.

Gladys laughs. Daniel laughs too.

DON (*Points to a picture*)   I notice a lot of the people who look through the window were payin' attention to this one . . .

DANIEL (*To Gladys*)   I'M JUST GOING TO LOOK AT THE PICTURES.

GLADYS   Well don't you have to—fix them up in—to get them the way you want it?

DANIEL   UM—NO! I'M GOING TO LOOK AT SOME OF THE PICTURES! THE PAINTINGS!

DON   This is my favorite. That's my mother. You see this macramé over here? She did that by hand, like when I was a kid, and I was always intrigued by that. And one day, she was gonna throw it out—

GLADYS (*Picks up a piece of cheese*)   Does anybody want some of this—stuff!

DANIEL   NO THANK YOU!

GLADYS   It's delicious!

DON   —and I said, "Why don't you just put it on the wall?" So I put it up for her, made a little frame for it, and then I figured, you know, thread *fades* . . .

66

DANIEL Uh-huh . . .

DON So I figured it's not gonna last forever, so I featured it in the picture. I painted the whole room, separately—and then I painted my mother while she was *in* the room. Everything you see is really there in real life. I tried to get the details right because that's what you remember when you think about something, so I tried like hell to get them the way they are.

DANIEL It's great . . .

GLADYS Honey? Do you want some? This—cook—cookie is absolutely delicious. Anybody want to try some?

DANIEL NO THANKS! IN A MINUTE!

Gladys starts humming.

DON Anyway, I don't know if you like that one . . .

DANIEL Did you—Did you mean to write three thousand dollars? These pictures are three thousand dollars apiece?

DON No, that one's three thousand, those over there are two, because that's a smaller canvas, and the rest of these are three.

DANIEL Gee, I hope you can sell them.

DON Well, first they gotta come in, right? (*Squints out the picture window.*) That couple's been by about five times now.

DANIEL I didn't know what time to come by.

DON Well, we been open for about four and a half, five hours—Since about eleven o'clock this morning. Not too many people came in yet, but it's so beautiful outside today. I tried to get my sister to come in, but it's a big ordeal for her to travel. She's pretty much a stay-at-home. And I don't get on too good with my brother-in-law. He takes good care of her, but he's—I don't know. He's always gotta be tellin' everybody what to do. He's one of those guys.

DANIEL When I was ten I broke my wrist outside on the hotel awning. Gladys was having a big opening for somebody and I went outside and I was playing tag with some kids, and I whipped around and ran right into the awning pole—and I cracked a bone in my wrist.

DON Oh yeah?

DANIEL (*Turning toward the desk*) And then another time I was in here, and she used to have a coffeemaker on the floor by the desk over there, and—

GLADYS How are you, honey?

DANIEL FINE THANKS.

GLADYS You havin' a good time? Did you look at the pictures?

DANIEL YES! I'M LOOKING AT THEM NOW! (*To Don*) And I kicked over the boiling water and it went all over my leg. Burned the shit out of me. I got all these blisters on my ankle. . . .

Pause.

DON Well, I'm pretty excited. I mean I don't usually get too excited, but this whole thing is kind of like a dream come true for me. You know, where I come from, in my town, you tell 'em you paint pictures and they look at you like you got a screw loose or something.

DANIEL Yeah, it's nice. This was a nice gallery.

DON Well, you know, Dan—I hope this isn't too presumptuous or anything, but I was thinkin', you know, you must know some of the people in the art department at your newspaper, and I was wondering if it wouldn't be too much trouble to put a bug in their ear and see if they could send somebody down to check out the show.

Pause.

DANIEL Well, um, Don—the thing is, I don't, uh, I don't actually work for a newspaper.

DON Because even a small blurb can make a big difference to a new show if it's in the *New York Times*. (*Pause*) What?

DANIEL I don't work for the *New York Times*.

DON Oh. Really? What paper do you work for?

DANIEL No—I don't work for a newspaper. I work for the Environmental Protection Agency . . . They don't have an art department.

DON	**DANIEL**
Didn't I hear Gladys ask you if you were still workin' at the *New York Times?*	Yeah, I know, I know, but I can't keep telling her—

And you said Yes!

DANIEL Don, I—I really don't work for the *New York Times*. I don't even have a subscription.

DON Oh. Huh. Well. I'm sorry. I—Phooey. Oh well. So you don't know anyone who . . . no, huh?

DANIEL Sorry. I wish I—

GLADYS Did you look at the pictures, honey?

DANIEL   YEAH, I THINK THEY'RE TERRIFIC.

GLADYS   Would you like me to buy one for you? I think one of these little ones would look just—in your place—in the—do you have pictures up in there?

DANIEL   Yeah, I have a lot!

GLADYS   I've never seen that one. That place in there.

DANIEL   What do you mean? You've seen it a million times!

GLADYS   I've never been in there.

DANIEL   Sure you have. You were in there last week!

GLADYS   Which one do you like, honey? Tell me which—tell me the—the show you like, and I'll fix it up for you. I want to buy it for you.

DANIEL (*Unsure if he wants a picture*)   Well—LET ME LOOK SOME MORE AND I'LL LET YOU KNOW!

GLADYS   Your mother bought two of them—

DANIEL   I KNOW! (*To Don*) Oh, did she buy another two, or . . .

DON   No, no, from when they were in here in the fall.

DANIEL   Oh yeah, they got 'em for my stepbrother.

DON   Did his wife have the baby?

DANIEL   Yeah, a girl. She had her last month.

DON   I've never been married.

Brief silence.

Ellen comes in.

ELLEN Hello.

DON Welcome back.

GLADYS Look, Ellen's here!

ELLEN (*A joke, to Daniel & Don*) Did you recognize me?

DANIEL Yup.

ELLEN Any customers?

DON Not yet, but I think people are really out enjoying the weather today. A lot of people are lookin' in, but I think they'll probably come in more after the weekend.

ELLEN I'm going to take her home, she must be exhausted.

DON Yeah, she's been talkin' a mile a minute since we got here this morning.

ELLEN (*To Daniel*) Where's your young lady friend? Didn't you say she might—

DANIEL Yeah, she had something to do.

ELLEN Is that situation any better?

DANIEL Well, yesterday it was.

ELLEN Oh dear . . . Not easy.

DANIEL That's right.

ELLEN Well, I'm gonna take her home—(*Goes to Gladys*) HELLO. WOULD YOU LIKE TO GO HOME?

GLADYS Sure, are we going to New York?

Ellen looks at Daniel, surprised and distressed by this new low.

ELLEN (*To Gladys*)   No—We're *in* New York. I said do you want to go home, to your apartment?

No response. Ellen looks at Daniel again, worried, and then back at Gladys.

ELLEN   IT'S ALMOST TIME FOR DINNER. WHY DON'T YOU LET ME TAKE YOU HOME.

GLADYS   I had no idea it was so late! Are you tired, honey?

ELLEN   No, it's not late, but it's time to go home!

GLADYS   All right, let me find my purse—

ELLEN   Your purse is on the back of the chair!

GLADYS   Wait—I don't have my keys—

ELLEN   I have your keys, I have them right here.

GLADYS (*Looks through her bag*)   Wait a minute, let me make sure I've got everything. I don't know where I put my— (*She dumps her purse out on the desk.*)

ELLEN   There she goes.

Gladys looks through her stuff.

DANIEL   Mom, I'm gonna go talk to Mr. George.

ELLEN   Well, honey, I already talked to him—

DANIEL   Well let me just try. I'm gonna call him and go see him and see if he can—I mean, she's not gonna be able to—

ELLEN   Well good then, go talk to him. There's certainly nothing to *lose* . . .

DANIEL   Yeah, because this is just awful—I mean—I—

DON   What are you gonna try to get him to let us stay open?

DANIEL   Well, I thought I'd go see if I can get another year out of him, because what difference would it make? And she can't—She's got to have something to *do*.

ELLEN (*Sighs*)   Well, good luck.

DANIEL   Yeah, I know, but—

ELLEN (*To Gladys*)   WHAT ARE YOU LOOKING FOR? (*Pause*) WHAT ARE YOU LOOKING FOR?

GLADYS   I'm looking for my keys! I can't find them!

ELLEN (*Shows keys*)   Your keys are right here! I have them in my hand.

GLADYS   Oh! Where'd you find them?

ELLEN   You gave them to me this morning! COME ON. IT'S TIME TO GO HOME.

As Ellen helps Gladys with her belongings, and helps her up:

DON   Well, this is just great. I want to thank all of you, because this has been just tremendous for me. I know things are gonna work out now for me, because I really believe that if you want something bad enough, you can have it as long as you don't quit trying. I mean—Greenwich Village—New York City gallery. I've been waiting for this day my whole life.

ACT TWO, SCENE THREE

Ellen's living room. Gladys sits in a rocker. Ellen sits on the sofa looking through a mail-order catalogue. Daniel and Howard stand nearby.

DANIEL   It was *the* most depressing thing I ever saw. Nobody comes in all day long, she's behind the desk—oblivious, like she's hosting a party, and he's standing around eating *cheese* in this empty gallery and he says to us, "I've been waiting for this day *my whole life*." It was just—

HOWARD   Jesus Christ.

DANIEL   It was the most depressing thing I ever saw—

HOWARD   Jesus Christ. That *is* really depressing . . . Oy. I'm gonna call my folks. (*Takes a step*) Dan, I called my folks last night and my mother picked up, and she was very upset, crying—and she said, "I can't stand it anymore, he's terrible, he's driving me crazy, he won't listen to anybody, he's so awful . . ." So I said, "Listen, he's ninety-three years old. He's a little difficult. Put him on the phone." He gets on the phone, I say, "Listen, Dad, what's the matter? Mom seems very upset." He says, "*I'll* tell you what's the matter—I knew this marriage was a mistake sixty-three years ago. I'm leaving, I'm getting a divorce, and I'm moving to China." So what do you think of that?

DANIEL   Wow.

HOWARD (*Moving to exit*)   So things are good all over with the old folks, right? If you don't lose your marbles and one of you doesn't die young, you get old together and torture each other to death.

DANIEL   Great.

HOWARD   See if I can calm him down . . . So fucking crazy . . .

He exits. Gladys looks at the dog, offstage.

GLADYS   Look at the dog. Ellen. Look at the dog. She's showing off. Isn't that sweet? That is the sweetest little animal. Look, she knows we're talking about her. She's showing off.

DANIEL   She doesn't know we're talking about her, she's a dog!

GLADYS   I had a beautiful little dog. Did you ever meet my dog, honey?

DANIEL   Sure!

GLADYS   Do you remember her?

DANIEL   Of course I remember her.

GLADYS   What?

DANIEL   I said I REMEMBER HER.

GLADYS   You do? She was the sweetest little thing. Ellen, do you remember that little dog I had?

Ellen doesn't answer. She turns the page of her catalogue.

GLADYS   This one is a little devil. Always sniffin' around somewhere. Look, she has a—a paw. She's scared you're gonna put her out in the street. She's trying to sing to you. Look at her. Don't you think I should give her something?

ELLEN   NO!

GLADYS   All right. (*To Daniel*) Do you know how to cook?

DANIEL   (*Sighs*)   A little bit.

GLADYS   You do! That's wonderful. I never cooked much. In that place, I have a little—fire, and I make myself a little sandwich. Does Ellen like to cook?

Ellen puts down the catalogue.

GLADYS   Ellen? Do you know how to cook?

Pause. Ellen is really shocked.

ELLEN   I've been cooking you dinner here every Wednesday for twenty *years* . . . !

GLADYS (*Laughs*)   Well where did you learn how to fix it up? Who told you?

ELLEN   I think she's gotten worse.

DANIEL   Oh, Mom.

GLADYS   You know, that one—the one in the back—he says he's leaving because his mother doesn't want him to be here—

ELLEN (*On "want"*)   No, it's got nothing to do with his mother—

GLADYS   What?

ELLEN   He's leaving because the hotel is taking back the gallery!

GLADYS   Yes, I know that . . .

ELLEN   He has to go back because he doesn't have a job and you have to get out of the gallery.

GLADYS   Well, what am I going to *do* all day long?

Silence.

76

GLADYS   I can't stay cooped up in that place all day long by myself! I'll go crazy!

ELLEN   We can talk about that later.

GLADYS   I think I'm going to look around and set myself up in a . . . in a . . . in a . . .

ELLEN   See? She forgets a lot of words . . .

GLADYS   In a little—you know, maybe I can get some work as a lawyer in an office. I still have a—paper—a—passport—and I can do a little of it—I don't need much, but I have to get out and do *some*thing—

ELLEN   Let's just get the gallery settled first and then we can worry about that later.

GLADYS   I think I'll go talk to that one who runs the—the hotel. I know his daughter—

ELLEN   There's nothing to talk to him about—(*To Daniel*) By the way, did you ever call Mr. George? Or did you decide—

DANIEL   Yeah, no, I'm gonna try to go see him this week, but I don't know if it'll do any—

GLADYS   What?

ELLEN   There is nothing to talk to him about—

DANIEL   THERE'S PROBABLY NOTHING WE CAN DO. YOU DON'T HAVE A LEASE.

GLADYS   Well maybe you and I can set something up in that place in the back. Would you like that, honey?

DANIEL   Let's worry about one thing at a time!

GLADYS One thing at a time. You know, I think that's very smart. We'll do it one—word—at a time.

DANIEL Good!

GLADYS Good. (*Pause*) Look at the dog . . . Ohhhhh, look at the poor thing, she's hungry—

Gladys picks up a plate of crackers.

ELLEN DON'T *FEED* HER! SHE'S ALREADY EATEN! She's getting too FAT! DON'T *FEED* HER!

GLADYS Well why are you so angry?

Ellen gets up and grabs the plate.

ELLEN I TOLD YOU *TEN THOUSAND TIMES* NOT TO FEED HER! SHE'S TOO FAT AND SHE'S ALREADY *EATEN*!

DANIEL Mom! She can't help it!

ELLEN (*Starts to cry*) Well I can't help it either, I can't *stand* it! (*Ellen runs into the other room.*)

GLADYS (*Bursts into tears*) Why is she angry at me? What did I do?

DANIEL She's not angry, she's just tired. She doesn't want you to feed the dog.

GLADYS Well I'm not going to stay here if nobody wants me, I'll go home! (*Still crying, she gets up with great difficulty.*)

GLADYS I don't know why she's always so angry at me! What did I do? Why is she yelling at me? I don't understand!

DANIEL (*Calling*) Mom . . . !

GLADYS   I'm going home, I'm going to kill myself.

DANIEL   DON'T KILL YOURSELF.

GLADYS (*Looks for her purse*)   Well I can't stay cooped up in that apartment all day long! No one ever comes in there!

DANIEL   PLEASE SIT DOWN. IT'S ALL RIGHT, WE'LL FIND YOU SOMETHING ELSE TO DO—

GLADYS   I can't stand it in there and I don't want to come here if nobody wants me here. I'll go home and kill myself. Where's my purse? I lost my purse!

DANIEL   IT'S ON THE ARM OF YOUR CHAIR—

GLADYS   Why is Ellen so angry at me?

Ellen comes back in and stands there.

DANIEL   Will you tell her you're not mad at her!?

GLADYS   I can't find my keys! I lost my keys! I won't be able to get back in! What am I going to do? I won't have anywhere to sleep! I'll be sleeping on the street!

ELLEN (*Comes forward, softly*)   Your keys are in your bag. But you don't have to leave. Do you want some coffee?

GLADYS   I don't want to stay if you're going to yell at me! I don't know what I did!

ELLEN   I'm not yelling at you, everything's fine.

Howard enters.

GLADYS   I want to get another—place—He won't take the pictures down, he says he's going *home*!

The doorbell rings.

GLADYS	ELLEN
And if he leaves the pictures up I can't *do* it by myself—	Hold on a minute, sit down, I have to get the door. Howard will you get the *door*?
I don't understand. What's the matter?	DANIEL
	I'll get it!

ELLEN I have to get the doorbell! Just wait one second!

GLADYS	DANIEL (*Going*)
I can't find my money—	Mom, I'm *getting* it!

ELLEN You don't need any money. That's Don and he's going to take you home in a taxi.

GLADYS Does he know the way?

ELLEN Yes, he knows the way—

GLADYS But I haven't got my keys!

ELLEN (*Looking through Gladys' bag*) I'm just finding them, they're in your bag.

HOWARD ELLEN IS FINDING THEM!

Daniel brings Don in.

DANIEL Hi, we're having a little scene here.

DON Oh, that's all right.

GLADYS I don't understand anything. I can't go home without my keys!

ELLEN (*Waving the keys*) Here they are. They're right here. Don't cry. Your keys are right here. Stop crying.

The keys are on an elastic bracelet. Ellen puts them on Gladys' wrist.

GLADYS   What?

ELLEN   There's nothing to cry about.

GLADYS   What's wrong with crying?

HOWARD   NOTHING.

ELLEN Sit down and take your time. Look, Don's here now, and he's going to take you home in a taxi. I'll call you in the morning when you're feeling better.	**HOWARD** (*To Don*) Hello. **DON** Hi there. **HOWARD** Just another evening at the Fine house.
GLADYS I can't breathe.	**DON** Yeah . . .

ELLEN   Because you're in a panic.

GLADYS   I am in a panic. I can't breathe . . . I'm dizzy . . .

ELLEN   Just sit down. Nothing's wrong with you, you're just upset.

GLADYS (*Sitting*)   All right, I'll sit down. (*She bursts into tears again.*)

ELLEN   Come on, don't cry . . .

GLADYS (*Getting up again*)   I don't want to go out on the street!

ELLEN   Nobody's going on the street. You're going to settle down and then Don is going to take you home in a taxi and I'll talk to you tomorrow.

GLADYS   Where's my bag?

ELLEN It's right here.

GLADYS
I had a coat when I came
in.

ELLEN
No you didn't. It's very
warm out. You didn't
bring a coat.

GLADYS
I didn't?

ELLEN
No.

GLADYS
Well now I upset you.

ELLEN
I'm not upset. You are.

GLADYS
Yes. I am upset. I'm sorry,
honey. I'm all mixed up.

ELLEN
It's all right.

HOWARD (*To Don*)
Was the traffic bad
coming up? Did you
take a taxi, or did
you drive your car?

DON
No, I took a taxi
because you can't get
a parking space down
there if you wait too
late . . .

HOWARD
All right. We'll
refund you.

DON
Oh, that's all right.
You don't have to—

HOWARD
Don't be ridiculous.
We'll pay for it.

DON
Well, uh . . .

GLADYS (*To Don*) Hello. We're having a—(*Makes a fist*) a
punch-up. (*She laughs*)

ELLEN "Ha ha ha."

DON Hello, Gladys!

GLADYS What did he say?

ELLEN He said hello. Now, do you have everything?

GLADYS Yes. Where are my keys?

ELLEN Around your wrist.

GLADYS (*Rattling them*) Oh here they are. (*Laughs*) They're right here.

Silence.

GLADYS What's everyone so upset about?

HOWARD WE'RE UPSET BECAUSE IT'S A SHAME ABOUT THE GALLERY.

GLADYS We'll I'm upset too!

HOWARD IT WAS A WONDERFUL PLACE FOR YOU BUT IT'S BEEN VERY DIFFICULT FOR YOU TO MANAGE LATELY!

ELLEN Don't shout, Howard.

HOWARD BUT IT WAS A WONDERFUL PLACE AND YOU HAD A LOT OF GOOD YEARS THERE.

GLADYS Yes I did.

HOWARD LISTEN, IT'S NO FUN TO GET OLD.

GLADYS What?

HOWARD I SAID IT'S NO FUN GETTING OLD!

GLADYS Well why do you always say that to me? Nobody wants to hear that—!

HOWARD (*Surprised*) I'M SORRY. I GUESS I'M NOT SO TACTFUL. I won't say it anymore.

GLADYS "You're old! You're getting old!" That's not a helpful thing to say.

HOWARD I—I'm sorry. Sometimes I'm not so smart.

GLADYS Sure you're smart! This whole family's smart! (*To Don*) Do you have money for a taxi?

DON Yep, right here.

GLADYS I'm very angry at you.

DON I just got here.

HOWARD That doesn't matter!

DANIEL (*Kissing her*) Bye, Grandma.

GLADYS Good-bye, honey. When will I see you?

DANIEL I'll see you tomorrow.

GLADYS Do you want a ride with us? Are you going to the city?

DANIEL No—We're *in* the city. I'm going home on my bicycle.

GLADYS But if you came with us, you could ride in a taxicab.

DANIEL I want to take my bike, I like riding it!

GLADYS All right. (*To Ellen*) He says he wants to ride his bicycle.

ELLEN Yes, I heard him. I'm standing right here. (*Kisses Gladys*)

GLADYS Good-bye, honey.

ELLEN I'll call you tomorrow.

GLADYS (*To Don*) What are *you* upset about?

DON I'm not upset.

HOWARD Gladys, *you're* upset!

GLADYS I am upset. I'm all—mixed up. (*She starts to cry again*) I don't want to stay in that place with those women! They don't talk to you and I don't know what to say to them! They sit there all day long and they never say two words to anybody!

ELLEN We can talk about it tomorrow.

GLADYS I don't understand what happened! Herb and I had a *good* life! We had a good life . . . !

HOWARD Yes you did.

GLADYS I don't understand what happened to me . . .

ELLEN Don't cry. We'll figure something out tomorrow.

GLADYS Tomorrow. All right. I'm very upset.

Gladys and Don go out.

HOWARD Good night, Don.

DON (*Off*) So long . . .

Ellen closes the door. Pause.

ELLEN I know everybody has to get *old* . . .

She stops talking. They all stand by the door for a moment.

ACT TWO, SCENE FOUR

Daniel comes forward.

DANIEL (*To the audience*)   I did go to see Mr. George. I asked him for another year. Just one more year before he took away the gallery, because after that it wouldn't make any difference anymore. And I thought it would make a great difference now.

    He was very sympathetic. He said he had an aunt who was going through the same thing. But he told me the same thing he told my mother on the phone. The cafe was scheduled to open *that* summer, and there was absolutely nothing he could do about it.

    Then he asked if we'd given any thought to putting Gladys in a home. I got kind of angry and I said we didn't really want to do that. She didn't like old people. She liked to be where the action was. She thought she was running a gallery. He said this is really the time her family should be taking care of her. (*Pause*) There were no more attempts to dissuade him.

    I kept thinking there must be something we could do, only I just couldn't think of what it was. I had a dream where I put her on a bus from Vermont to New York, and I wanted to get her settled and get off, but as she hobbled down the aisle I was afraid she'd be knocked over by the bus's motion, and it occurred to me that she'd never know where to change buses, that it was impossible to put her on a bus by herself because she'd never make it. But I couldn't go with her and was all too late. Her mind was smashed to pieces, and the person she used to be hadn't really been around for a long time. . . . But the pieces were still *her* pieces. (*Pause*) I guess we all wanted to get out of it.

*As a clock chimes twelve, the lights rise on the hallway between
Gladys' and Daniel's apartments. Gladys, wearing an old housecoat,
slowly walks to Daniel's door and rings the bell, a loud horrible electric
buzzer of a doorbell. Pause. She rings it again. Pause. She turns
around and starts to walk slowly back to her door.*

Daniel, half asleep, opens his door, putting on a bathrobe.

DANIEL HELLO . . . !

GLADYS (*Turning*) Hello? Hello?

DANIEL HELLO. WHAT'S THE MATTER?

GLADYS Ohhhhh, I'm sorry, sweetie, did I wake you?

DANIEL YES!

GLADYS Ohhhhh, I'm sorry. I tried to ring your doorbell
yesterday and nobody was there. I didn't know where you
were. I was worried. You weren't home.

DANIEL So *what*?

GLADYS
Well I didn't know where
you were. Where is your
mother? I tried to call
her but she's not home.

DANIEL
I'm here *now*—and
Mom is asleep—You
probably—

GLADYS What, honey?

DANIEL (*Slowly and distinctly*) You probably misdialed. Mom
is probably asleep. It's after midnight.

GLADYS Oh, do you want to come in and sit down?

DANIEL NO. I WANT TO GO BACK TO SLEEP. IT'S
VERY LATE.

GLADYS Oh. All right. I'm awfully sorry I woke you, honey.

DANIEL That's OK.

GLADYS Are you like me? Can you go right back to sleep?

DANIEL YES.

GLADYS All right, honey, I'm sorry.

DANIEL IT'S ALL RIGHT.

He goes back inside. She goes very slowly inside her apartment. Muffled and distant, the church bells chime three o'clock. Gladys comes back out, fully dressed, carrying her purse. She rings Daniel's bell. Pause. She rings again. Daniel jerks open the door, hair rumpled, in his underwear.

GLADYS What's the matter, honey, is the house burning down?

DANIEL What?

GLADYS Is the house burning down?

DANIEL No.

GLADYS Where did your mother go, honey? Is she in your apartment?

DANIEL No!

GLADYS
Well why didn't she say good-bye to me! She was here before and then she ran out and she didn't say good-bye! I don't know where she went! Why did she leave like that? What did I do to her?

DANIEL
What? Mom wasn't here!

No—No—Listen a —*Listen* a minute!

88

DANIEL   She hasn't been here for hours! She was here last night—LAST NIGHT!

GLADYS   But why didn't she say good-bye?!

DANIEL   She *did* say good-bye. She said good-bye last night! And now it's after midnight and she's home asleep!

GLADYS   No!

DANIEL   YES! SHE WAS HERE BEFORE AND SHE SAID GOOD-BYE AND NOW IT'S AFTER MIDNIGHT!

GLADYS   Well why did she run out like that? I thought we were going to the country!

DANIEL   NO! YOU'RE MIXED UP! NOBODY'S GOING TO THE COUNTRY!

GLADYS   *They* don't have to invite me! I'll just stay here by myself!

DANIEL   THEY'RE NOT IN THE COUNTRY!

GLADYS   But where are they?

DANIEL   AT HOME IN BED!

GLADYS   Why? What time is it?

DANIEL   IT IS THREE O'CLOCK IN THE MORNING!

GLADYS (*Hand to mouth, shocked*)   I had no idea it was so late.

DANIEL   WELL, IT IS.

GLADYS (*Bursts into tears*)   But why didn't your mother tell me she was leaving!

DANIEL   SHE *DID* TELL YOU! SHE *DID* TELL YOU!

GLADYS   NO! SHE NEVER TOLD ME ANYTHING—!

DANIEL YES SHE *DID*!

GLADYS NO!

DANIEL YOU NEVER BELIEVE *ANYBODY*!

GLADYS BUT SHE NEVER TOLD ME SHE WAS LEAVING!

Daniel actually slams his own head into his front door. Gladys gasps and takes a step back.

DANIEL MOM IS ASLEEP! HOWARD IS ASLEEP! IT IS THREE O'CLOCK IN THE MORNING! (*Pause. Slightly calmer*) THEY WERE HERE LAST NIGHT. THEY SAID GOOD-BYE, AND YOU'RE GOING UP THERE FOR DINNER ON WEDNESDAY!

GLADYS You're very angry.

DANIEL No, but I'M TRYING TO GET SOME SLEEP!

GLADYS What's the matter, honey? Are you having trouble sleeping?

Daniel starts to answer. He half-laughs.

GLADYS I thought Ellen was mad at me.

DANIEL NO. NOBODY'S MAD AT ANYBODY.

GLADYS Well that's all I care about. Do you want to come inside for a minute?

DANIEL NO, I WANT TO GO BACK TO SLEEP. IT'S VERY LATE AT NIGHT. YOU SHOULD TRY TO SLEEP ALSO! AND I'LL SEE YOU LATER.

GLADYS All right, honey. I'm sorry.

DANIEL It's all right!

Gladys turns around and walks slowly to her door. Daniel turns and goes inside his apartment as she goes inside hers. Pause. The distant clock chimes five.

GLADYS (*Off*)   Help! Help! Somebody help me!

Gladys comes out from her apartment, and goes toward vestibule door.

GLADYS   Help! Help! Somebody stole my dog! Help! Help!

Daniel opens his door and runs out, tying his bathrobe around him.

GLADYS   Honey help me, somebody stole my dog! They ran out into the street and—

DANIEL   Grandma—

GLADYS   —I can't find her anywhere! I think somebody stole her!

DANIEL   Grandma, you don't have a dog—

GLADYS   What are you talking about! She's gone!

DANIEL   Nobody stole your dog. She died a long time ago. You're having a bad dream.

GLADYS   But they were just in here—

DANIEL   Who was in here?

GLADYS
Billy and Pearl—They
were in here two minutes
ago and they ran out, and
the dog ran out, and I
can't *find* her!

DANIEL
No! Listen to me—
PLEASE LISTEN TO ME!

GLADYS   I'm listening.

DANIEL   You are having a dream. The dog died many years ago. Billy and Pearl are in Fairfield, in Connecticut.

91

They've been there for fifteen years, they weren't here. You've been having a bad dream.

GLADYS   Do you want to go upstairs and check?

DANIEL   No. It's five o'clock in the morning, nobody is here but you and me, there's no dog. There is no dog.

GLADYS   Are you sure?

DANIEL   Yes.

GLADYS   (*Doubtful*)   Well, all right . . .

DANIEL   Come into your apartment. Did you eat anything yesterday?

He takes her into her apartment as they talk. The lights go up in her living room.

DANIEL   Sometimes when you don't eat you get a little confused. I want you to eat something—

GLADYS   But I'm not hungry, I have to fix something for the people to eat for dinner—I can't—

DANIEL   No, nobody is coming for dinner. It's very early in the morning and I want you to eat something. Sit down here. Sit down. SIT DOWN.

GLADYS   But they'll be looking for me—!

DANIEL   NO! NOBODY'S LOOKING FOR YOU! SIT DOWN!

She sits in a chair. He exits.

GLADYS   Maybe you should check upstairs. I think something happened to them. There were—three of them, and they came in and they—(*She stares at the empty chair.*) Where—

Daniel enters with a bowl of yogurt. He puts it in front of her.

GLADYS   Is he going to get coffee? Oh, no, I couldn't eat anything, I'm not hungry!

DANIEL   Just eat this—please!

GLADYS   But I'm not hungry!

DANIEL   IF YOU DON'T EAT THIS I'M GOING TO KILL MYSELF!

GLADYS   But I *can't*—!

DANIEL   PLEASE PLEASE PLEASE PLEASE PLEASE PLEASE EAT THIS! *PLEASE!*

He's screaming so much she starts eating.

GLADYS   This is delicious.

DANIEL   Good.

GLADYS   It's very good. (*She eats*) So what's new with you, honey? Are you working hard?

Daniel laughs.

GLADYS   Are you still working for the—the television?

DANIEL   Yes!

GLADYS   For the magazine? And people call you and you bring them here and fix up what you want them to do for you?

DANIEL   Yes.

GLADYS   What are you doing now?

DANIEL   Um, I'm—

GLADYS   (*Twists around*)   Where did he go?

Pause.

DANIEL Who?

GLADYS (*Points at an empty chair*) Didn't you see him?

DANIEL (*Very rattled*) Who? There's nobody there.

GLADYS He was sitting right there, just a minute ago. Your—Herb! Your *brother*. Where did he go?

Pause.

DANIEL He—he's not here.

GLADYS What?

Daniel looks at her for a long moment.

DANIEL He'll be back later.

GLADYS Do you want me to give him a message for you?

DANIEL Um—

Gladys' voice has now dropped to a normal level we haven't heard before. She seems calmer and more self-possessed, more like her old self must have been once. She seems to have momentarily crossed over to another place altogether. She speaks as if Daniel is just one of three or four people in the room with whom she is talking.

GLADYS I used to work for Herb in that lab, you know, when Herb and I were living in Germany. We used to play tennis and go dancing—and it was really rather nice. But that was when the Nazis were marchin' around all over the place, so after a while we decided to get the hell out of there and come home.

DANIEL Can you understand me?

Gladys looks right at him, but it's impossible to tell who or what she is really seeing or hearing.

GLADYS   What?

DANIEL   Can you understand what I'm saying?

GLADYS   I don't know. I never knew what I was doing . . . !

Daniel gets up and goes to the phone. Gladys does not notice.

GLADYS   But when we got to that train station, they were all there to stamp your ticket, and he takes my ticket and he looks at me and he says, "Bist du judische?" Do you know what that means? It means "Are you Jewish?" And I looked at him and I said, "Ich spreche kein Deutsche"—"I don't speak German." (*Pause*) But when I took Ellen down South to visit Herb at that army base, it was so damn hot down there, all you could do is sit on the porch and fan yourself! There was no one to talk to. Everyone needs someone to talk to, otherwise you'd just go nutty. I love to talk to people.

Daniel dials the phone.

GLADYS   I'm havin' a good time!

Daniel starts crying suddenly and keeps dialing.

GLADYS   Everybody likes to have a good time. What's wrong with that? (*She eats.*)

DANIEL (*on the phone*)
Mom. Hi, it's me, I'm
sorry to wake you—
Well I don't know. She's
completely out of her
mind. She's hallucinating
I don't know what, and
she's literally talking
nonstop. I haven't

GLADYS
We never did what any-
body told us! We used
to sneak out of the
house all the time!
We'd go up to Harlem
to hear music, we'd
go out dancing . . . We

95

slept in three days, she wakes me five times a night, and she never, never stops ringing my doorbell. And I can't take it anymore. I'm really sorry. (*He starts crying again*) Can you come get her? . . . OK. Yeah. All right. I'm really sorry. (*He hangs up*)

had a marvelous time. We really did. Now, I used to play a lot of tennis, but I was never very good at it. I just played it for fun. You know. But Jean was a wonderful tennis player, oh, she was marvelous. And you know Ellen was a wonderful tennis player when she was a teenager. Oh, everybody likes to do those things. Nobody likes sittin' around in a stuffy old house with a lot of boring people. You know?

Daniel sits on the sofa.

GLADYS But Ellen's always been shy, poor thing. We were so happy when she married Mark because he's had a rough time, he really has. You can't spend all your time running around, nobody'll know what you're talking about!

Daniel shuts his eyes.

GLADYS But Mark is very charming, he works very hard, he's a hell of a nice guy, and he's a damn good doctor. (*To Daniel*) You're a good doctor.

The lights fade out. The distant clock chimes eight times.

ACT TWO, SCENE FIVE

The lights come up on Daniel, asleep on the sofa. Gladys is offstage. We can just hear her talking steadily in her sleep.

GLADYS (*Murmurs indistinctly offstage*) . . . There were the four of us. My sisters, Harriet and Jean, and there was Harold, of course. He was the youngest. And we had a big old house out in Brooklyn. Of course this was a long time ago . . .

Ellen uses her key to come into the apartment. Daniel wakes up with a start.

ELLEN Hello.

DANIEL Oh—Hi.

ELLEN Did you get any sleep?

DANIEL Not really. I was afraid she would wander outside . . . She finally went to sleep an hour ago . . . Except she's been talking in her sleep nonstop . . . Man, she sure does like to talk.

ELLEN Oh dear. I'm sorry, Danny. I feel just terrible. We'll take her for a few days and let you get some sleep.

DANIEL (*Yawning*) Yeah, I could really use it . . .

Ellen walks around the room.

ELLEN I really think we're going to have to move her in with us after the summer. She can't stay here anymore. And if we can rent this place out as an office, we could get a couple of thousand bucks for it and use the money to hire somebody around the clock, because this is really no good . . . Anyway, why don't you go in your apartment and get some sleep.

DANIEL Yeah, all right.

Pause.

ELLEN   How are things with you and that girl? You said she . . .

DANIEL   Um, yeah, she started dating one of my friends.

ELLEN   Oh dear.

DANIEL   She says that my feelings for her are not her issue.

ELLEN   Not her what?

DANIEL   I don't know. I don't really want to talk about it.

ELLEN   OK . . .

DANIEL   I guess I'll give her one more try and then give up.

GLADYS (*Murmurs offstage*)   . . . We were very lucky. Our parents gave us a wonderful education . . . We went to museums and concerts and galleries . . . I never liked school very much, I was always sneakin' off to the library to read plays . . .

She trails off.

DANIEL   She spent the whole night talking about Herb and Harold and her sisters . . .

ELLEN   It's all *in* there, I guess. It's just . . . it's just all— jumbled up . . . (*Pause*) I *wish*—she would just die peacefully in her sleep, but Dr. Wagner says there's nothing wrong with her physically. She could go on like this for another ten years . . .

DANIEL   Great.

GLADYS (*Murmurs offstage*)   . . . Well, we were very anxious, naturally, because nobody ever explained it to us and we just didn't know what to do . . .

ELLEN   I wonder what she *thinks*. If she thinks anything.

DANIEL   I don't know . . .

ELLEN   Well . . . when I get senile just put a bullet through my head.

There is a startled pause.

DANIEL   You won't get senile.

Silence. Don lets himself into the apartment with a key.

DON   Oh—Good morning.

ELLEN   Good morning.

DON   Anything the matter?

ELLEN   No, nothing. She had a bad night, so I'm gonna take her uptown for a few days . . .

DON   Oh. Oh.

ELLEN   How are you?

DON   Uh . . . well, not so good to tell you the honest truth— uh—

ELLEN   Why? What's the m—

DON   —somebody smashed the windows in my car last night.

ELLEN & DANIEL   What?

DON	**DANIEL**
Somebody smashed all my windows—	What is going *on*?
	ELLEN (*With Daniel*) I *saw* a bunch of windows smashed up—

DON Yeah! I just went to move my car and three of the windows were smashed in. I asked the doorman in front of the building on the corner if he saw what happened and he said the night guy told him some kids came by last night in a limousine or somethin' and—

ELLEN Oh my God . . .

DON —and one of 'em jumped out of the car and—You want to get this? He smashed in the windows of a buncha cars with one of those—with a giant-sized bottle of champagne.

ELLEN Are you serious?

DON Yeah! The guy just went up and down the street smashin' in windows, jumps back in the limousine and drives away down the street.

DANIEL Jesus Christ.

DON Do you believe that? I mean, what the hell is *that*?

ELLEN Did anybody *see* them?

DON Yeah somebody saw 'em, the night doorman saw the whole thing! He's the one who told the day guy about it. And I asked him, I said, "Why the heck didn't the guy *do* something? What, the guy just stands there and watches 'em breakin' everybody's windows?"

DANIEL Those cars get smashed all the time.

DON I don't even know if I'm covered for vandalism. I know I'm covered for theft . . . I . . . You know, Ellen, I don't want to let you down or anything, but I guess I've had it. I'm pretty optimistic by nature, but I gotta admit I'm very, very discouraged by this city. I mean, I surrender. You know? I gotta go home. I can't—I can't even afford this. You been great to me, but . . .

Silence.

ELLEN   I wouldn't think you could *break* a car window with a bottle.

DON   I guess those giant-sized bottles are made of pretty thick glass. Who knows? Anyway, I figured I'd tell Gladys I can't go to the gallery today. Cops said I should come in and file a report, but what the hell are *they* gonna do? They should talk to the friggin' night doorman, is what they should do. But . . .

Pause.

ELLEN   Well—you have keys to the gallery, right? So . . .

DON   Yeah, I'll pack the stuff up tomorrow morning. I might have to make two trips, but I'll let you know what I'm gonna do. Hope nobody hikes the car while it's sittin' there with no windows. I, uh—I'm feeling very depressed.

ELLEN   Well, I'm sorry. That's very unpleasant.

DANIEL   Yeah . . .

DON   I'll say it's unpleasant. (*Pause*) All right, so . . . Where's she gonna be, your house?

ELLEN   Yeah, for a few days at least, if you want to—

DON   OK, I'll swing by later and say good-bye to her, probably tomorrow . . . I'd sure like to get my hands on whoever it was . . . I don't know if they were white or black or what, but . . . They probably were *white*. I was always worried about these crazy drug guys. Just goes to show you . . .

ELLEN   Well—That is really revolting.

DON   Well—*I* don't live here.

ELLEN   OK, Don, see you later.

DANIEL   So long.

DON   Yeah, so long. (*He exits.*)

ELLEN   That is really charming . . .

GLADYS (*Off*)   Ohhhhhh! Ellen? Ellen? Where's Ellen?

They listen closely, thinking she's awake. Pause.

GLADYS (*Off, still asleep*)   I don't know when they're going to get there . . . We never did it that way before . . .

Ellen heads into Gladys' bedroom.

ACT TWO, SCENE SIX

Daniel comes forward. Behind him, Howard enters, carrying boxes. Under Daniel's speech, Ellen enters with Gladys, who is dressed in a coat. Ellen sits her down and puts her sneakers on for her as Howard moves boxes. (They are moving Gladys out.)

DANIEL (*To the audience*) After the summer was over, Mom and Howard moved Gladys out of her apartment and up to their building. When I went by the hotel in the fall, I saw that Mr. George had not yet begun construction in the gallery. It was exactly as Gladys had left it when we moved her out. Even her desk was still there . . . A year and a half later, he still hadn't begun construction, and when he finally did, the restaurant didn't actually open until two summers had gone by. And it wasn't a breakfast cafe, it was just a regular restaurant. It wasn't even attached to the rest of the hotel.

Pause. It seems like he has more to say, but he just stands there for a moment.

HOWARD Dan.

DANIEL (*Turns*) Yeah . . .

HOWARD Can you give me a hand with the door, dear?

Daniel opens the door for Howard, who goes out carrying a box.

HOWARD Thank you.

Ellen kneels in front of Gladys, takes off her slippers and puts on her shoes for her.

ELLEN (*To Gladys*) OK, WE'RE GOING TO GO NOW.

GLADYS Are we going to New York?

ELLEN   Yes. Come on. It's time to go.

GLADYS   Who's gonna keep an eye on the—Honey, who's gonna keep an eye on the basement?

ELLEN   WE'LL TAKE CARE OF THE APARTMENT. YOU DON'T HAVE TO WORRY ABOUT THAT ANYMORE.

GLADYS   Well he's worried because he doesn't have a place to stay in the summertime! Are you going to go back for the summer?

ELLEN   NO, IT'S OCTOBER NOW. WE'RE NOT GOING ANYWHERE.

GLADYS   There are two—places in the back. Have you seen those little places? I want to get out when the weather gets better and find myself a little job, because—

ELLEN   COME ON OUT TO THE CAR.

GLADYS   What's the matter? Where am I going?

ELLEN   We're all going uptown together!

GLADYS (*Beginning to panic*)   But where are you taking me? I can't go outside, I don't have any money!

ELLEN   You don't need any money. Howard and I are going uptown to MY house in the CAR.

GLADYS	ELLEN
No! I don't want to go! Why are you throwing me out?	It's all right, it's time to—

ELLEN   We're not throwing you out, we're all going together.

GLADYS (*Crying*)   But I don't want to go anywhere, I want to go to New York, I want to get a job!

ELLEN (*Walking her toward the door*)   We are going to New York! We're all going there now and we're going to have some dinner!

GLADYS   I don't *want* to go outside—I don't have any—*shoulder*—I don't have any *weapons*—Why are you trying to kill me?

ELLEN   Nobody is killing you. Howard will take you out to the car and I'll be right there and then we're going for a short trip in the car to my house, and we'll all be together the whole time. The car is right outside.

GLADYS   Are you going to Brooklyn? Is everybody going to Brooklyn?

HOWARD (*Gently takes her arm*)   WE'RE GOING UPTOWN TO OUR HOUSE. IT'S A VERY SHORT TRIP.

GLADYS (*Crying again*)   I don't want to go, I don't understand where you're taking me! I don't want to go by myself!

HOWARD   We'll be with you the whole time. Keep walking.

GLADYS   Keep walking. I don't even know where I'm going! What did I ever do to you?

HOWARD   You didn't do anything and nothing bad is going to happen.

GLADYS   I don't want to go! Where's Ellen? I don't understand why I have to go! I want to paint that place and sell it to the real estate and nobody ever *listens to me*! Wait—wait—I don't have my keys!

HOWARD   YOUR KEYS ARE IN YOUR BAG!

ELLEN   They're around her wrist.

HOWARD   YOU DON'T NEED ANY KEYS—

ELLEN (*Stepping up to her*)   Your keys are around your wrist.
HERE. HERE. BUT YOU DON'T NEED THEM
BECAUSE YOU'RE GOING TO STAY WITH US
FROM NOW ON.

GLADYS   I don't want to go with you, I want to find my own
apartment and I want to get a *job*!

ELLEN   WE CAN TALK ABOUT THAT LATER.

GLADYS   I don't understand where you're taking me!

HOWARD   You'll see where you are when you get there!

Howard takes Gladys out.

GLADYS (*Off*)   No! No! I don't want to go with you! I don't
want to go!

Ellen shuts the door. Silence.

ELLEN   Oy. All right. (*Pause*) Do you have the lamp?

DANIEL   Yeah, you gave it to me this morning.

ELLEN   OK. And you don't want the . . . bureau, no, that's
for Annie . . .

Silence. Ellen looks around the room.

ELLEN   This place looks really dismal.

DANIEL   Are you gonna fix it up before you try to rent it? or . . .

ELLEN   Oh yes, we have to, the whole ceiling looks like it's
about to come down. (*Pause*) I don't know. I feel so awful. I
feel so dismal and hopeless. I don't know what's going to
happen to her but I wish it would just happen. (*Pause*) I

know she always drove me crazy, but she was never a bad person. She was very loving. And she always wished me well.

DANIEL I love you, Mom.

ELLEN I love you too, sweetheart.

Ellen starts crying. They put their arms around each other.

ELLEN I came down here in the spring one time, and I caught up with her as she was on her way to the gallery . . . And she was crawling along at a snail's pace, and her ankles looked so skinny, they were like *tooth*picks—and she just looked like this skinny old lady on the street, she looked as though a wind could blow her over. (*Pause*) She doesn't understand what's happening to her and neither do I . . . !

DANIEL Mom, I love you so much I can't even tell you. I don't know what I'd do . . .

After a moment, she pulls away.

ELLEN All right. I don't want to leave poor Howard with her alone in the car.

DANIEL All right, I'll see you for dinner tomorrow.

ELLEN All right, sweetheart. Ay yai yai. Maybe we'll all survive.

She kisses him. Pause.

ELLEN I think this really did me in. (*Pause*) Let me know if you change your mind about the bureau.

DANIEL OK, Mom, I'll see you tomorrow.

ELLEN Good-bye, sweetheart.

She goes out. Daniel comes forward.

DANIEL (*To the audience*)   Gladys moved in with Mom and Howard, where she just got worse and worse. For the last two months of her life all she did was moan, whether she was awake or asleep. A friend of mine said the whole thing was just unanswerable, and I guess it was. After she moved uptown, I would see her when I went to visit, but I was out of it now.

My mother never got out. With the help of Howard, Florence and Marva, she heroically stood by Gladys for the next two years. She took care of her and dressed her and cleaned her up and fed her and watched her fall apart, day in and day out with nothing to stop it and no relief in sight.

One night Mom called me up and told me she thought Gladys was dying. I rode my bike uptown and went into the back room where Gladys lived now. By that time she was just this tiny, eighty-seven-year-old body, lying in the back of her daughter's apartment, hanging on with almost nothing, but struggling anyway for one more breath.

She finally died around two in the morning. And after that, it was a lot easier to remember what she was like before. But I never want to forget what happened to her. I want to remember every detail, because it really happened to her, and it seems like somebody should remember it.

It's not true that if you try hard enough you'll prevail in the end. Because so many people try so hard, and they don't prevail. But they keep trying. They keep struggling. And they love each other so much; it makes you think it must be worth a lot to be alive.

He exits as the lights fade out.

THE END